"There are lots of books on content marketing, but here's why you should buy this one: it's been proven in the trenches, generating tens of millions of visitors for real businesses. You know who else can say that? Nobody." – JON MORROW, SMARTBLOGGER.COM

"A practical, simple, accessible guide to an effective content marketing program. And that's the highest praise I know." – ANN HANDLEY, AUTHOR *Everybody Writes: Your Go-To Guide to Creating Ridiculously Good Content*, CHIEF CONTENT OFFICER, MARKETINGPROFS

"Content is not a tactic — it's air for marketers. This book will help you master the art of content and, perhaps more importantly, help you breathe easier doing it." – JOHN JANTSCH, AUTHOR OF *Duct Tape Marketing* AND *The Referral Engine*

"Creating really good content isn't easy, but Pamela Wilson has written the definitive book on how to get it done. Clear action steps, a solid business strategy, and a simple, realistic process will have you creating high-quality content on a consistent basis. Anyone who needs to write effective content — whether or not you think of yourself as a writer — needs to pick up this book." – SONIA SIMONE, CHIEF CONTENT OFFICER, RAINMAKER DIGITAL AND COPYBLOGGER

"There are only three books I keep on my desk: a thesaurus, a book on grammar, and now *Master Content Marketing*. This practical book easily leads you through all the steps to create revenue-boosting content. When you have a conundrum, dip in and quickly find the fix. Pamela's bright, can-do attitude will lift you up, giving you skill and confidence as your content marketing soars to new heights." – KARYN GREENSTREET, SMALL BUSINESS STRATEGIST, PASSIONFORBUSINESS.COM

"If you've ever thought marketing wasn't for you, if you've ever felt funny promoting yourself or your work, or maybe wondered if there was a better way to do it, then this book is for you." – JEFF GOINS, BEST-SELLING AUTHOR OF *The Art of Work*

"This is perhaps the most actionable book on content creation and marketing I've ever read. Every single page is filled with formulas, checklists or tools to use, all in a blueprint-like order that can't be screwed up. If you're new to content marketing, you'll be dog-earing every other page." – JOANNA WIEBE, COPYHACKERS

"Here's the problem with most marketing books; they contain many ideas but no clear path on how to put those ideas to use. You won't have to worry about that with *Master Content Marketing*. Pamela not only shares the ideas but the exact process, strategy, and system to make content marketing doable and fun — even if you don't consider yourself a writer! Congratulations, you've just found your go-to resource for building your online presence." – DAVE CHAREST, SENIOR MANAGER, CONTENT AND SOCIAL MEDIA MARKETING, CONSTANT CONTACT

"In an increasingly noisy online world, it's still possible to build a successful business with content marketing ... if you do it the right way. Pamela's book will help you discover how to create content that will attract and retain an audience, and enjoy yourself along the way. I've built a multi-six-figure business based on these principles, so I know it works!" – JOANNA PENN, BESTSELLING AUTHOR, AWARD-WINNING ENTREPRENEUR, TheCreativePenn.com

"This book cuts through the fluff and teaches you how to create good content consistently. I especially like Pamela Wilson's "lazy" approach—she understands we have lots of other to-dos on our plate, and her time-saving tips make content creation feel doable, even for the busiest solopreneurs." – HENNEKE DUISTERMAAT, FOUNDER OF ENCHANTING MARKETING

"Whether you like it or not, your business is now competing in a world of competing content. That means even if you don't write it yourself, you need more and more content, and it needs to have the right impact. I have witnessed Pamela help businesses break through their content blocks in person, and on webinars. I have no doubt the wisdom she has distilled within these pages will do the same for many more people." – CHRIS GARRETT, CO-AUTHOR OF *Problogger: Secrets for Blogging Your Way to a Six-Figure Income*, AND CHIEF MARKETING TECHNOLOGIST, RAINMAKER DIGITAL

"*Master Content Marketing* is the step-by-step instruction manual you will want to have at your fingertips every time you create a new piece of content. Even if you don't consider yourself a writer, this system makes content marketing totally manageable. Best of all, it's a fun book to read – filled with great stories and illustrations." –BETH HAYDEN, CONTENT MARKETING STRATEGIST, BethHayden.com

"In today's age, if you can't master content marketing, you won't have a business. Pamela Wilson did the hard work of cutting through the chaos and overwhelm of advice, sharing only the best, tested, actionable tools to grow your tribe and drive revenue to your business." – PAMELA SLIM, AUTHOR, *Escape from Cubicle Nation, Body of Work*

MASTER CONTENT MARKETING

A Simple Strategy to
Cure the Blank Page Blues and
Attract a Profitable Audience

Meet Your Guide

This owl will lead you through the information in *Master Content Marketing*. Watch it get smarter (just like you!) as you go through the book.

A Simple Strategy to
Cure the Blank Page Blues and
Attract a Profitable Audience

Pamela Wilson

Foreword by Brian Clark

BIG Brand Books
NASHVILLE, TN | 2016

Print edition
ISBN 978-0-9978754-0-9

Designed and produced by Pamela Wilson, Big Brand System

Illustrations by DJ Billings, aka Sparky Firepants

Edited by Afterwords Communications

Contents

Foreword

You're holding an important book in your hands. Let me explain why.

Back in the Internet dark ages of 1998, I started publishing online, hoping to make a living as a writer via this new medium. And I fortunately began by doing something that is now critical to modern marketing — I built an audience.

What I did wrong was try to make money selling advertising. It's a tough game even today, so you can imagine how difficult the late 90s were for new digital publishers.

I soon discovered that attracting an audience with valuable free content in order to sell products and services was the much smarter approach. And that's the definition of content marketing.

One could argue, however, that at this point you can just call it *marketing*. Content has become so indispensable to reaching the right people online that it is simply accepted as a given.

Back when I got started, we basically figured things out by trial and error. There were no how-to books, courses, or conferences. Many mistakes were made and hard lessons learned.

After starting three successful businesses by building audiences between 1999 and 2005, I decided to start a site that shared what I had learned. Copyblogger launched in January of 2006, and as far as I can tell, it was the earliest site about what we came to call content marketing, and it remains the largest.

Nowadays, we might have the opposite problem of my early learning curve.
Scores of people profess to be content marketing experts. Who can you trust?

You can trust Pamela Wilson.

Pamela started contributing to Copyblogger in 2010, and built her business just like we had built ours — by creating compelling content that attracted the right people for our products and services. She was such a consistent contributor that she felt like part of the Copyblogger family, so I was delighted when she accepted my offer to *run* Copyblogger.

Now *that's* trust.

I handed over the keys to the megasite I had founded without hesitation. Pamela was now in charge of an audience of hundreds of thousands of people that had helped me grow Rainmaker Digital to a $12-million-a-year business — without venture capital or advertising.

And that's why it's fortunate that you've selected *Master Content Marketing: A Simple Strategy to Cure the Blank Page Blues and Attract a Profitable Audience* to be your guide. Because Pamela knows what she's talking about, period.

The title of the book reveals three important aspects of content marketing that works:

The first of these is *audience,* which we've touched on. Content marketing is not about "campaigns" that are really poorly-disguised pitches. You create the right kind of content that attracts the right kind of audience, resulting in more customers and clients.

Next is the word *strategy.* Research on content marketing effectiveness shows that the people who struggle with it have no documented strategy whatsoever. Reading this book will immediately put you on the right track, because you'll understand exactly what you're trying to accomplish before creating a single piece of content.

Finally, the third important word is *simple.* No respectable book on content marketing would claim that it's easy … you're effectively becoming a media producer with a smart content strategy, and that takes work.

And yet, the fundamentals of content marketing are simple, and it's important to have a guide that clearly and concisely communicates those fundamentals. That's also not an easy task, and Pamela has done it.

Enough from me, let's dig in. I owe my entrepreneurial and small business success to content marketing, and I wish the same (and more) for you.

BRIAN CLARK
Founder and CEO, Rainmaker Digital
Boulder, CO – August 31, 2016

Prologue

If You're Not a Writer, This Book is for You

I'm not a writer either. Wait! Where are you going? Let me explain.

I'm not a *born* writer. I became a writer — quite late in my career — out of a desire to share what I'd learned over my decades in business. Until 2010, the longest text I'd ever written were love letters to former boyfriends and long emails to clients of my design and marketing firm.

The idea of sharing my writing in public — where anyone could read it — terrified me.

But something happened between then and now. Along the way, this non-writer developed some techniques and shortcuts for writing that worked every time.

Much to my surprise, I became a person who could reliably write — for my own business, and now for others' businesses.

It all started when I made the decision to write on a regular basis, despite feeling completely unprepared for the task. This book will show you how to write successfully online and do it confidently and consistently. And it will serve as an ongoing companion and reference guide as you write to attract prospects and turn them into customers and advocates.

Writers Aren't Born; They're Self-Made

This book will challenge the notion that writers are born especially blessed with verbal virtuosity.

I'm here to tell you that good writers are deliberate about their writing. They take it seriously. They make time to do it regularly. They study the art and craft of writing, and they write — a lot.

They also use structure in their writing. You may not see that structure now. In this book, I'll show you how to recognize it — and how to use it yourself.

As you read on, you'll see that I don't assume any prior knowledge of writing or content marketing. If you're starting completely from scratch, welcome — you're in the right place. And if you have some experience, I'm hoping that the tips and techniques I'll share — which I use while managing the content on one of the most-respected websites in the world — will prove valuable.

You'll walk away from this book with both a recommended structure for effective content marketing and some ideas for developing the habits that will make creating it a natural part of your work life.

Do You Have an Idea Worth Spreading? Write!

Maybe you're reading this because you already have a topic you're passionate about. You have an idea, an approach to a challenge, or some inspiring words you want to share with the world.

You may have heard about "content marketing" and you want to use it. As you should! It's an effective — and cost-effective — way to spread your ideas.

We'll talk about content marketing in the next chapter. For now, know that almost all content marketing starts with the written word. Even video and audio have an underlying structure that starts in written form. Mastering the art of expressing your ideas with the right words will help get them out into the world faster.

My "Lazy" (But Efficient!) Approach to Content Marketing

When I started my brand new blog, Big Brand System, I knew that it was only by writing and publishing on a regular basis that my site was going to get recognition on-line. Why? Because I wasn't going to have any face-to-face interaction with the customers of my online business. No handshakes were going to happen. No meetings over coffee. No conference room presentations. How would they learn to trust me?

*One way to build trust when your business is virtual is to publish consistently
useful content on a reliable schedule. In other words, show up and be helpful,
week after week.*

I decided my publishing schedule would consist of one good post every single week, without fail.

Now, that's not a terribly ambitious plan by some standards. Next to people who publish three, five, or more articles every week, publishing once a week is a lazy schedule! But at the time, I was also running a booming full-time business. My two children were still living at home and I had numerous community commitments. With everything else going on in my life, one good blog post every single week didn't seem lazy — it seemed close to impossible.

But the more I researched successful online marketing, the more I realized that publishing one post per week was the least I could do if I wanted to make an impact.

And I did want to make an impact. Don't you? I'll bet that's why you're here, reading this book. Making an impact with your content is what this book is about.

So I focused on learning how to create content *efficiently*. I developed systems that worked for me — systems that were fast, repeatable, and effective. I did it in the name of publishing content the "lazy" way, with a schedule that worked for me and helped me achieve my business goals.

*The "lazy" approach means developing labor-saving techniques for getting things
done so you have more time for other areas of your life.*

You're about to master the easiest system I know for creating consistently readable, informative, and effective content. I'm going to show you how to write content that makes an impact every single time. Even if you think you're not qualified to be a writer.

Keep Learning – for Free – When You Register

*Before you do anything else, be sure to visit MasterContentMarketing.com/bonus
to register for the free content marketing tools and resources I've created for you.
They'll help you make the most of everything you're about to learn.*

Soon there will be no more staring at the blank page, cursing the cursor that's blink-blink-blinking back at you. Those days are over.

But first, I should tell you how I managed to figure this system out.

Setting Yourself Up for Content Marketing Success

CHAPTER 1

Old Marketing is Dead: Why You Should Master a Better Kind of Marketing

Back in 2009, I was sitting right where you are today. I knew (vaguely) that "content marketing" was the best way to reach people online. But me? Writing content myself? It was laughable.

I was a trained *designer*. When people approached me for marketing help, I came up with a plan, hired a writer to create the words we needed, and then did all the design work to make their marketing ideas come alive. I didn't write — I made other people's writing look good.

Plus, there were lots of reasons to avoid writing online where anyone could read it.

- **Loss of privacy:** When your name appears as the author of a piece of writing, everyone can see it.
- **Feeling judged:** When your work is out there in public, people may or may not like what you wrote (and they'll tell you about it!).
- **Not feeling capable:** When you're first starting out, you lack experience. What if your content isn't good enough?
- **Concern it won't pay off:** You might fear that even though you pour your time and energy into this, you won't see results.

With all these worries rumbling around in my head, I did what anyone would do. I opened Google. And I searched for "online content." And guess what site came up? Copyblogger.com.

This was late 2009, just as I was formulating my idea for an online business that would teach marketing and design basics people could apply to their businesses. And since Copyblogger effectively does what I am about to show you, I had stumbled upon one of the top content marketing resources on the web. Copyblogger had been around for years at this point. I should have found it before, but I wasn't looking for it before!

It was a perfect example of the student being ready and the teacher appearing.

I devoured everything I could on the Copyblogger blog. I even signed up for Copyblogger's premium course at the time, Teaching Sells. In that class, I discovered how to leverage my professional knowledge by packaging it into an online course and selling it for a profit.

I'd been working as a traditional marketer for decades at this point. You know how marketing was done traditionally, right? Some people call it "spray and pray."

You'd blanket a target audience with what amounted to advertising. You hoped (prayed) that a large enough percentage of them would "take the bait" and respond to your offer.

I was one of the people behind those direct mail postcards you'd find in your mailbox. I designed those brochures you were given by the company that wanted your business. I put together the annual report that tried to convince you that you'd made a smart investment. I assembled those magazines that pushed ad after ad for products that companies hoped (prayed) you'd remember when you got to the store.

I created *a lot* of trash. Oh, it wasn't trash right away. It served a purpose. Temporarily. But once its purpose was fulfilled, off to the landfill it went.

Why? Because none of the traditional marketing I did had any *intrinsic value*. No one was saving it, bookmarking it, and coming back to it to read it again.

What I discovered very quickly about content marketing was that it was *valuable*. The first time someone told me, "I've saved every newsletter you've sent," I knew I was on to something.

Content marketing was a different — and better — kind of marketing.

Instead of pushing messages out at unsuspecting people, content marketing offers valuable information that people are actively searching for. What a difference!

Why "Spray and Pray" Doesn't Work Anymore

Everything has changed since my early days as a marketer. When I started, the internet wasn't even around. Marketing had a handful of avenues where it could reach you:

- Your mailbox
- Your driveway (in the form of a newspaper)
- In stores (as magazines for sale)
- In places of business (as flyers, brochures, or printed coupons)
- Over the airwaves (in the form of radio and TV advertising)

And that's about it. Oh sure, there was the occasional blimp floating by, or the person wearing a sandwich board at an intersection. But not much more than that.

Marketing was pushed out at you — whether you liked it or not — in all these places.

You didn't ask for the direct mail to land in your mailbox. You didn't want the commercials on the radio. You may have subscribed to the newspapers or magazines, but it was for their content, not their ads.

Let's look at that last line again:

You may have subscribed to the newspapers or magazines, but it was for their content, not their ads.

From the very beginning, it was *content* that was considered valuable. It still is. Advertising was (and still is) regarded as a nuisance.

What Kind of Marketing Works Now

With the advent of the internet, a seismic shift has happened. Consumers now hold the power during the purchasing process. Instead of waiting to see which ad catches their attention, they go in search of answers. They arm themselves with information so they can make a qualified decision.

And those of us who want to market our products and services serve up the information they're searching for in the form of readable, friendly content. Our content gives a face to our businesses and establishes a trustworthy relationship by serving as a helpful guide.

Content marketing is like putting out bait rather than throwing a spear.

Old marketing? It was like throwing marketing "spears" at a school of fish in the hopes you'd hit one. You wasted a lot of energy and didn't see a lot of results.

Content marketing? It's like offering some delicious, nutritious bait, and inviting the fish to swim your way. It draws them in. The best part is that some will stay there, interacting with your brand. They'll become your customers, and then repeat customers.

Sounds good, doesn't it? I know I'd much rather be creating useful information than blanketing people with ads. Wouldn't you?

From Reluctant Writer to Content Marketing Teacher

One decision I made early on was to reach out to the owners of websites that were serving an audience that was similar to the one I wanted to serve. This is an effective way to broaden your reach, especially in the early days of your website.

It's called "borrowing someone else's audience," and is otherwise known as guest blogging. Looking back, I'm not sure how I found the courage to approach the team at Copyblogger with a guest post I'd written. At that point, I'd only been writing content for a few months.

But during a concert I attended, I had a moment of divine inspiration that resulted in writing a post I was proud of. So I sent it off to the then-editors of the Copyblogger blog and crossed my fingers and toes while I waited for a reply.

A few days later, when I saw the email in my inbox letting me know they liked my post and planned to publish it, I was overjoyed. When the post was published, it ran with a different headline and some edits to the content. Rather than feel bad about the changes, I noted them and decided to learn from the edits they made. Then I found the courage to send them a second post a couple of weeks later.

This went on for a few months — they'd publish a post, and I'd send them a replacement post. Eventually, I was asked to contribute a post to the Copyblogger blog once a month. And today, I hold the record for the most posts from an outside writer.

We enjoyed working together so much that I was invited to join the team at Copyblogger — now Rainmaker Digital — in 2014.

And just five short years after I submitted by first guest post to the editors at

Copyblogger, I began running the editorial team for the Copyblogger blog, which is one of the largest and most respected content marketing resources in the world. Along with our editor and staff writers, I help set the direction for the content we publish every single day.

And I teach content marketing! I believe starting as someone who didn't consider herself a writer gives me an advantage as a teacher.

Those early days of content marketing weren't easy. I still remember publishing my first, my fifth, and my tenth blog posts. It was nerve-wracking, and not just because I thought I might make a grammar or spelling mistake. It was because I had no idea how to structure and present my thoughts.

That's Me – Now Back to You and Your Writing Journey

It turns out that once you have a structure to hang your words on, creating content becomes much easier. Once you know how to write and polish the essential elements of a successful piece of content, you'll be able to create effective content for your business reliably.

And when you combine solid content structure with habits that will help you develop lifelong writing skills? Well, watch out, world!

This is when content marketing becomes fun. Something you'll look forward to. Something you'll find yourself thinking about as you go through the paces of your everyday life.

You'll see a concert, and it will inspire a piece of content. You'll meet a new business colleague, and a question they ask you will inspire a piece of content. You'll take a trip, and you'll come up with the topic for a new piece of content.

Suddenly, the world around you will become living inspiration for the content you've got inside you that's waiting to get out. With the powerful combination of a content structure and reliable content habits, there will be no stopping you.

Taming the Content Monster with Structure and Process

But if you haven't created content before, the thought of building content to attract people to your website might be a wee bit overwhelming, despite my reassurances.

I get it. I've been there. Remember, I wasn't born a writer! And yet, I figured out how to make it easier by applying both structure and process to content creation. I'm about to show you how it works.

In the next chapter, we'll start by talking about how to set yourself up for content creation success — with a "lazy" (but efficient!) approach that makes content creation a fun part of what you do every week.

Then we'll cover how to plan the content you'll write, and I'll show you a simple system you can use to map out content ideas.

Let's begin mastering the content marketing process, so you can create effective content consistently over time. Because it's only through consistent content publishing over time that you'll see real results.

CHAPTER 2

The Efficient Approach to Marketing Your Business with Content

If you could see me as I type this, you'd see that I'm gleefully rubbing my hands in anticipation. Because in this chapter, we're going to set out toward the heart of this book. We're going to start talking about how to build out the content on your website. And I'll begin to share my system that you can use to make this work efficient, effective, and — dare I say it? — fun.

> *Content marketing works when you create useful, interesting, and engaging information consistently over time. It's all about showing up reliably and being helpful every single time.*

Sounds daunting, doesn't it? Are you wondering what in the world you've signed up for? Well, don't worry. From here on out, everything in this book is designed to teach you an efficient approach to your ongoing content creation process. Because if you're going to use content to market your business, you're going to need to be in it for the long haul. We're going to make your journey as pleasant and productive as possible.

Why Aspire to the "Lazy" Approach?

I'd like to share a new way to think about the word lazy. In my experience, people who look like they're working less than the rest of us have often found smart ways to make their work more efficient and faster to accomplish. That's the "lazy" approach we'll explore here.

Here's what the "lazy" approach gets right:

"Lazy" people don't reinvent the wheel each time they perform a task. Instead, they identify a process that works for them, and they stick to it. They don't let new tools or new ways of doing things distract them from getting the work done.

"Lazy" people put effort where it counts and nowhere else. They don't spin their wheels overdoing some tasks and under-doing others. They identify how much effort each task requires and give it what it needs and nothing more.

"Lazy" people have rituals and habits. Rather than rely on pure willpower (or looming deadlines) to get their work done, "lazy" people build their ongoing work into their daily and weekly schedule in a way that makes doing it seem like a natural part of their lives — not something they have to force themselves to do.

How to Set Yourself Up for Efficient Content Creation

It's just us here, so let's be perfectly honest. "Lazy" content creation is appealing to you, isn't it? So let's explore how you can become the "laziest" and *most efficient* content creator out there. It all starts with setting up an environment where "lazy efficiency" can flourish.

Creating content on a regular basis is less painful when you don't have to force yourself to do it. Think about everything you do on a daily and weekly basis to make your life function efficiently:

- You bathe
- You eat meals
- You brush your teeth
- You shop for food
- You wash your clothing

Now that you're an adult, you don't have to plan any of these things or figure out how to do them. You probably do them the same way every time. They're a natural part of your day or your week.

You don't resist them or procrastinate about doing them for the most part. (I'll confess that I procrastinate about grocery shopping until I've run out of things to make for dinner. That's when I know it's time to re-stock the shelves.)

Why do you do them so effortlessly? Because whether you recognize it or not, you've already got *systems* in place for getting them done. When it's time to brush your teeth, your toothbrush and toothpaste are in the same spot they've always been. All you have to do is grab them and begin. There's no resistance to the task because it's frictionless: simple, easy, and efficient.

How to Make Content Creation Frictionless (and Fun)

It may be difficult to believe, but content creation can be just as frictionless as all of the tasks above. This section will help you identify how to set up a physical and mental environment that will make the process easy and natural for you. Content creation is both a physical and mental task, so it's important to plan for both aspects.

Once your physical environment is prepped and ready, you'll be able to create content the same way you brush your teeth: you'll have what you need right at hand so you can grab it and get started. And once we've worked on your mindset, you'll find your mental environment will be prepped and ready for you to dive into your content creation process, too.

Your Ideal Physical Writing Environment

It's funny to me that I've never heard anyone address the physical aspect of content creation. Let's face it: we can't just *think* our content into existence, can we? We have to sit or stand and place our fingers on a keyboard or pen to paper and begin physically writing the words that will make up our content. This happens in a space and in a moment in time. Let's talk about both.

Your ideal physical writing environment:

Is a place where you're physically comfortable. Your chair supports you, and you can easily reach your keyboard or your notepad without scrunching up your shoulders or craning your neck. If you stand, you have a supportive surface below your feet and good shoes, so your legs and back don't suffer.

Is a spot with the best light for you. You recreate the lighting that works for you. Some people focus best in a dark "cave," with shades drawn and a single light illuminating their work surface. Others feel more productive with bright natural light. Identify what lighting setup helps you do your best work. When it's time to create your content, make lighting part of the setup.

Is convenient and nearby. You'll resist your content creation tasks less if you don't have to travel to get to the place where you'll create content. Find a spot that's already close by, and designate it as your content creation station.

Has everything you need within arm's reach. My content creation station is a red reclining chair in the corner of my office with a small blanket I can throw over me if I get chilly. On the small table next to this chair, I have a place to set my coffee cup; a pencil and pad for notes; a tissue box; and some lip balm. I write on a computer and have a thesaurus and dictionary just a few clicks away. Your setup will look different than mine. Content creation is a job like any other job; put your tools together, so they're within easy reach.

Features sound — or the sound of silence. Some people prefer a little background noise (or music), and others need complete silence. What works best for you? Pay attention, and make what you hear part of your setup.

Is distraction-free. When it's time to create content, you'll get more done if you shut down distracting websites and social media sites, and silence your phone.

Your Ideal Time of Day for Creating Content

Content creation also happens at a moment in time. For most of us, our mental energy runs in a predictable daily cycle. We're most efficient around the same times every day.

Sometimes we have no choice — it's a matter of working around our other responsibilities. If you have young children, for example, your efficiency may increase dramatically the moment they lie down to go to sleep at night!

If you haven't identified your peak creative times of day yet, I'd like you to pay attention to this over the next few weeks. At what time of day does creative work seem to come easily to you? And when does your brain consistently feel like mush — like you couldn't get an original thought out of it even if you squeezed it?

There's no right or wrong answer here. I want you to find *your time,* not anyone else's. Once you pinpoint your peak creative time, plan to use at least part of it for content creation. When you do this, you'll find putting together your content will be easier, faster, and more efficient.

Does Everything Have to be "Perfect" to Create Your Content?

Do you *have* to be in that ideal physical environment and in the middle of your peak creative time in order to create content?

Absolutely not. I've done enough writing at hotel desks and in plane seats to attest to the fact that great content can come out of a variety of environments and times of day.

What we're talking about here is how to set up a frictionless environment and time-frame for *most* of your daily or weekly content creation work. You'll find that once you've set yourself up in a supportive environment and found a time slot that works for you, content creation will become more of a habit than a to-do item.

Habits done in one place can easily be transferred elsewhere.

If you're staying in a hotel, you can still brush your teeth, right? And it's still auto-matic because you've trained your body to grab what you need and get the job done. Do the same for your content creation process, and you'll find it's easier to make it happen no matter where you are.

Why Does Creating Content Become More Fun Over Time?

Content marketing offers those of us who don't feel as if we've been blessed with the mythical writing gene an opportunity to improve our skills one piece of content at a time.

Think about it: if you want to learn to cook, you start with the basics. How to boil water. How to make toast. As you master these basic skills, you enjoy the fruits of your labors: you eat the broth you boiled or chew the toast you made.

It's the same thing with content. Even your earliest attempts at published content will work for your business. As long as it's carefully crafted (more on that later), search engines will begin to find it and lend authority to your site. It doesn't have to be a mas-terpiece to benefit your business.

But as you write more, something will occur naturally. Just like practicing cooking over time will allow you to make more complex and delicious dishes you can then eat and enjoy, consistently creating content will help you build your mastery. You'll find you can go from idea to finished product faster and more smoothly. You'll know you can count on your content creation skills to create ever more sophisticated content marketing for your business.

It may come as no surprise, then, that content creation tends to become more fun over time. That's the effect mastery has! When you've built your skills and they've become a resource you can easily draw on, you enjoy the process — you even look forward to it.

That's why I'd like you to look at your content as if it's a *body of work* you're going to create. To understand this concept, let's chat about Pablo Picasso, my favorite artist.

The Picasso School of Content Creation

Whether or not you admire Pablo Picasso's work, you have to admire his approach to his craft.

He was a one-man art *factory*. Over his lifetime, he produced 50,000 paintings, drawings, etchings, sculptures, ceramics, and prints. That's approximately 632 pieces of art for every year of his 79-year career.

Because I love his work, I've seen a fair amount of it in person. Whenever I travel, if there's a Picasso in a museum nearby, I make a side trip so I can see it in person.

Seeing art in real life is a much richer experience than seeing a reproduction in a book. You're able to perceive the artist's creative process. With Picasso, you can often see his brushstrokes and sometimes even his fingerprints.

After decades of looking at Picasso's work in person, I began to notice something.

Not everything Picasso created turned out to be a masterpiece. Some of it looks like nothing more than a failed experiment.

When you see enough of Picasso's work, you note that sometimes, he wasn't quite able to express himself clearly. But as you continue to look at his work, you also recognize that it was constantly evolving. He'd begin to explore a style or technique, and push its limits a little more with each new piece he created.

You'll have your fair share of failed content experiments, too. And when those failures happen, I want you to think like Picasso — tomorrow is another day, and you'll have another chance to get it right.

How to See Your Content as a Body of Work

Over time, every piece of content you create will be a step in your evolution as a content creator. No single piece of content is going to define you or your business. Some pieces will be more successful than others, and that's perfectly fine.

So don't put pressure on yourself — or your content — to make it "perfect." Think of every piece of content as one more addition to the gallery of content you're building. Each step forward is building on the one before. And the more you create, the better you'll become — you can count on that.

Content Creation Habits That Grow Your Body of Work

Let's imagine Picasso's typical day. I am making this up from my imagination and — as you'll soon see — adapting it to fit our topic.

Pablo wakes from a restful sleep and sees the light coming through his curtains. He thinks about what he'll work on that day, building anticipation for the creative projects ahead. As he pads into his kitchen, he makes a first cup of coffee and greets the day. He's going to go into "Creation Mode" soon and doesn't trouble himself thinking about the world's problems or his personal challenges. He's preparing his mind to be open, relaxed, and ready to create. His routine relies on the "lazy" habits he's developed.

His first "lazy" habit is to move into his physical creative space — in this case, his studio. He sees that he's left his tools out where he needs them the evening before. This allows him to move directly into his warm up without distracting himself with, say, checking email or social media sites. (I told you I was making this up!)

"Lazy" habit number two: Pablo picks up his tools and begins to warm up. He dips a brush into some leftover paint from his latest project and makes marks on a piece of brown craft paper. He's not expecting anything to come from this warm up. He's quietly preparing his body and his mind to switch into creative work. For ten to fifteen minutes, he makes lines, shapes, and textures on his large piece of brown paper. At one point, he paints a curvy shape that reminds him of a reclining woman.

"Hmm," he thinks. "That's interesting. I wonder where I could take that idea?"

He knows it's almost time to begin his creative work because his brain is now sending him ideas he'd like to pursue. So he moves over to his "real" tools: his full range of paints, multiple brush sizes, and his pre-stretched canvases. He takes out a pencil and lightly sketches the curvy shape along one edge. Creation Mode has begun.

Do you see how Picasso eased himself into his creative work? He had a warm-up session where he had set up a frictionless environment (a space devoted to doing the work and all the tools set out the day before). He placed no expectations on an outcome from the work. His only goal was to warm up his creative mind.

In that judgment-free place, when his physical body was already in position to do something about it, his creative mind offered up an idea.

This is how content creation works. When you put yourself in the physical space where you create content, then suspend all judgment about the outcome and *just write,* amazing things happen. It's like your mind says, "Oh, you're ready for me now? OK, here goes!" and it sends you ideas you can act on.

That's why I get impatient with people who say, "I don't create content because I never know what to write about." Content creation is a *habit* you form. Part of the process is setting up your physical environment for success — carving out a space and laying out your tools. The other part of the process is withholding judgment on the outcome.

Plan for a warm-up period at the beginning of each content creation session. *Write anything.* Put your fingers on your keyboard or pen to paper and form words. Any words. It doesn't matter if they don't make sense. Remember, you're using leftover paint on brown craft paper. You're just warming up and putting yourself in the best possible physical and mental place to move into Creation Mode.

Don't think too much. Just write.

The best ideas come from a place in your mind that's not standing in judgment or full of worry. It's not distracted or stressed. It's relaxed and looking forward to *just doing the work,* in happy anticipation of the process more than the final product.

When you get yourself to this place — and I promise if you put in a few weeks of consistent practice you'll get there — you'll look forward to this creative time. Creating content will be a joyful job you'll want to do often.

But for content marketing to build your business over time, you'll need your body of work to reflect your business goals. That's what we'll talk about in the next chapter: how to look at your content as a story you'll tell about your business, your customers, and their challenges and questions. You'll discover how to map out a plan that will guide your content creation for years to come.

The Efficient Approach to
Marketing Your Business with Content: A Checklist

☐ **Recognize that it's a journey, not a destination.** The results from content marketing happen when you create compelling information consistently over time. When you set yourself up for success, you'll look forward to this creative task.

☐ **Embrace a "lazy" approach.** The "lazy" approach means making content creation easier by setting up a frictionless environment for getting your work done. "Lazy" = efficient and smart!

☐ **Find a place where you're physically comfortable.** Make it somewhere you can count on being able to work most days.

☐ **Use the best light for you.** Identify the lighting you prefer, and find a way to reproduce it consistently.

☐ **Put everything you need within arm's reach.** Keep it all at hand so you don't interrupt your work session looking for something you're missing.

☐ **Identify your most creative time of day.** Take it from me; it's *much* easier to do creative work when you're working inside your most creative time of day. Pinpoint your ideal time, and block out part of it for content creation.

☐ **Don't judge. Just do.** Like an artist, incorporate a warm-up period where you write about anything that comes to mind. This will help prepare your mind and body for the creative work to come.

CHAPTER 3

Online Content Marketing Strategy: How to Plan the Content You'll Write

Let's pretend we're going out to dinner together and I've just told you about a new restaurant I want us to try. Your first question to me is, "What kind of food do they serve?"

And my answer is, "Well, their sushi is fantastic. Their lasagne is better than my mother's. And their tacos are to die for."

Strange, right? Is it a Japanese, Italian, or Mexican restaurant? Or is it just a confused restaurant?

When people come to your website, their mind is full of questions. But the number one question in their minds is, "What will I find here for me?" or "What's in it for me?" (as we say in the marketing world).

People don't usually surf the web with altruistic goals in mind. They're looking for something for themselves.

And when they arrive on your website, they want to know if you have what they want.

That's why it's important to have a cohesive "menu" of information on your site just like a restaurant needs a cohesive menu of food.

You want to present a business story that's clear and easy to understand. You want your value to shine through immediately. You want to answer the "What will I find here for me?" question clearly and quickly.

This isn't as hard as it might sound. Remember that at your favorite restaurant, somebody at some point sat down and made decisions about the overall style of food they'd serve. Then they developed individual categories for their food, like Appetizers, Soups, Salads, Fish, Meat, Poultry, Pasta, Side Dishes, Desserts, and Beverages. Within each category of food, they developed dishes they knew their customers would love.

This is what we're going to do for your website in this chapter. We'll develop a menu that will meet the needs of your customers with your content. Once you know the topic you want to be known for, you'll develop categories for it. And once you've got those categories set up, you'll find interesting ways to pair items together to make a memorable information "meal" for your site visitors.

How to Tell a Cohesive Story with Your Content

What kind of "restaurant" do you want to run? What kind of content will you serve up?

And will it be a fast food joint where people can quickly fill up a hungry stomach with food that — although it might not be very nutritious — does the job? Or will it be the kind of place people tell their friends about? A place that's so unique and memorable that it becomes a beloved part of the community — a hub where people gather, share stories, and get their fill of nutritious, delicious, beautifully prepared information? A place where they can count on learning more about a particular topic from a trusted authority in the space?

I hope you aspire to the latter. When your content works well, your website becomes that kind of "restaurant." It has a cohesive, memorable story. It becomes a destination where people go to fill up on helpful information. And they tell their friends about your business.

A cohesive story is an easier story to remember and share.

Doing this takes time and involves some pre-planning, but it's worth the effort. This plan will help keep your website on track and ensure that you tell a consistent story over time. It will keep you from developing a taco dish and putting it on the menu at your sushi restaurant — and confusing your customers completely!

Categories Keep Your Story Consistent

One important feature of content management systems — software like WordPress that helps you to easily add content to your website — is the ability to add categories to the content you create. Categories help your readers to find related information on your website.

One of the smartest things you can do — even if your site is established — is to set up clean, clear categories you'll fit your content into.

Content creation happens over time — lots of time. And it's tough to keep your content goals at the top of your mind every day for a year, five years, ten years. Categories help with this: when you set them up right, they provide a guide for the content you'll create. They help you when you're planning content and when you're writing it. But most importantly, categories help your readers.

When a reader comes to your website and reads an article they enjoy and find helpful, they may want to see what else you've written about the same topic. This is where a simple click on a category link has the powerful effect of taking them to a page that serves up more of the same. It's a little like allowing a restaurant customer to sample one dessert and then rolling up a cart with all the other desserts you have available. You've given them a taste, they enjoyed it, and now they want more.

The Set It and Forget It Plan for Category Creation

You know what often happens as people put content onto a website? They write about a new topic they've never covered before. And they assume (often wrongly) that they're going to be writing about this topic a lot in the future. So they create a new category for it.

Then, something surprising happens. Maybe their audience doesn't respond much to the new topic. They don't comment, share, or visit that article. Or the writer loses interest in the topic. Or the topic becomes outdated because of new technology. For whatever reason, the new category languishes with only one or two posts.

This is a huge mistake. It's confusing to readers when a site has too many categories. And the categories begin to lose their ability to guide the content creator's work because they're too varied and random.

Let's avoid this fate with some careful planning. Let's think ahead and set up categories that will work for you now and in the future. And then let's forget all about them so we resist the urge to add categories continually and dilute their guiding power.

Aim for Eight to Ten Categories Total

I recommend you don't feature more than eight to ten categories total for your website. Most content marketing systems also offer tags, which we'll talk about below. Tags don't need to be as limited and can be more specific than categories. If you're feeling fenced in by only eight to ten categories, tags will help.

One way to approach this is to set up four to five categories to start. Give yourself space to expand your content into additional categories as time goes on and you see patterns to the kind of information you want to add to your website.

How will you find the perfect categories for your content? Here are some tips:

Choose words your audience uses, not you. Category names aren't a place to be clever or obscure. Avoid professional jargon your audience won't understand. Think about the kinds of keywords they might type into a search engine to look for the information you'll feature on your site, and use these words as categories. Let's look at some examples.

Imagine a website for a business that offers courses and coaching for young engineers. Remember, we don't need to use "engineers" in all our category names: this is assumed since it's the topic of the whole site. This website might have categories like:

- Job hunting
- First job tips for engineers
- Continuing education
- Time management
- Promotion tips

For a new site, these categories might be enough. Starting with five gives the content creator space to expand into other categories as their goals become clearer.

Most content management systems also include the ability to apply tags to content along with categories. If categories create broad subtopics you'll organize your content under, where do tags fit?

Pick broad categories and get specific with tags. Categories are like the sections on your menu, and tags are more like individual ingredients in the dishes you offer. So aim for categories that describe the general type of content. Use tags to describe ingredients *inside* that content. Let's expand on the example above by creating tags for topics that may have been mentioned inside an article with a couple of these categories.

Category: Job hunting.
Tags: resumés, interview tips, interview dress code

Category: Time management
Tags: to-do apps, time blocking, distractions

Just like the restaurant owner, planning your major categories in advance doesn't limit you to *only* using those categories. You can add to or edit them as you get to know your readers. It's a good idea to approach this content organization task as something you'll work on and tweak as time goes on.

And if you're just not sure about what categories to use, I'd like to ask you to make an educated guess. *Imagine* your readers if you don't have any yet. Try to put yourself in their shoes and think how they'll phrase their queries. What words will they use? How can you take those words and turn them into categories for your content?

Create Content Ideas for Each Category

The next step is to think through content that will fit under each category. At this stage, you don't need to imagine the headline for each piece of content, just the overall article concept.

To do this step, you can create a mind map with branches for each category. Add content ideas as sub-branches. Or, use index cards. Write the category name at the top, and fill in content ideas on the front and back of the card. Sticky notes can also work — just choose the medium that feels most comfortable to you.

If you have customers, start by writing down questions they always ask you about your topic. If you own a business with a customer service department or support team, tap them: they'll know the most common questions. Then ask yourself the three questions here to inspire content ideas:

1. If I was just learning about this topic, what would I want to know?
2. If I wanted to understand how to apply this information to my own situation,

what would I need to know?

3. If I wanted to become proficient on this topic, what information would I have to master?

I'll go into this in more detail in the next chapter. For now, remember the answers need to apply to the specific audience you want to write for. Let's look at our website for young engineers and answer these questions for the first category:

Category: Job hunting

1. If I was just learning about this topic, what would I want to know? *The best websites for young engineers to find a first job. Expected salary ranges for beginning engineers. What engineering jobs are really like.*
2. If I wanted to understand how to apply this information to my own situation, what would I need to know? *The top three questions engineers are asked in interviews. How to make up for lack of experience when applying for jobs. What to wear to an interview.*
3. If I wanted to become proficient on this topic, what information would I have to master? *How to negotiate a higher salary. Top ways to shorten the search and find a job quickly. How to network your way to a better job.*

At this stage, I recommend you leave your plan in plain view, whether it's a mind map open on your computer desktop, index cards on your desk, or sticky notes on a wall. Leave it out for a few days and revisit it often. Give your mind a chance to work on this task in the background. As you go about your day, you'll find content ideas bubbling up when you least expect them. Keeping your plan readily available will allow you to quickly add ideas as they occur to you.

Find Ideas by Cross-Linking Categories

Here's a fun way to come up with brand-new content ideas that fall solidly within the category structure you're aiming for. Take two of the categories on your list and combine them to come up with a new source of inspiration. Using our example, let's combine these two categories: **Job hunting + Time management**

Let's look at content ideas that may come up from combining these two categories:

Job hunting + Time management: *How to find an engineering job in just one hour a day. Simple strategies for finding an engineering job when you already have one. How managing your time like a pro will help you find the engineering job of your dreams.*

Let's take another example so you can imagine how combining two categories can help you generate content ideas: **Continuing education + Promotion tips**

Continuing education + Promotion tips: *7 ways getting an MBA helps engineers to earn more. How engineers get ahead with online continuing education. A quick technique to pinpoint the exact course you need to take to move into your dream job position.*

Very quickly, you can see how adding two categories together helps you think about a whole new set of content ideas. And the beauty of this technique is that *you're still on topic.* You're not adding tacos to a sushi menu!

Think About Links

We're not going to delve deeply into search engine optimization in this book, but there is one thing I want to mention so you keep it in mind as you work on your content plan.

One of the smartest things you can do as you're creating your plan — and later as you're writing your content — is to think links. *Lots of links.* Links backward, links forward, links out, and links in. Let me explain:

Links backward. When you're writing a new piece of content, think about where you've already talked about the topic. (You'll write about some topics over and over, always from a slightly different angle.) Add links to previously written content as you write your new pieces. Think about foundational concepts people reading your current article might need to grasp before they can use the new information you're sharing. Link backward so they can educate themselves.

Links forward. One important reality of search engines is that they tend to assign higher rankings to content that has been around a while. Because of this, it's also important to go back to older content and "link forward" to newer articles. Find content that already ranks well, and edit it to add links to your newer content. In this way, your older content will help boost the rankings of your newer articles.

Links out. Remember that we're creating content because we want our websites to be seen as authoritative resources on our topic of choice. One aspect of being an authority figure is knowing who's who in your field and recommending reliable sources of information. As you write content, be sure to link out to other sites that complement what you write about. Doing so can help you get on the radar of other site owners, who should see notifications about your links. That may help you with the next idea ...

Links in. As your site becomes established, part of your job is to encourage other sites to link to yours. These "inbound links" will help people browsing other sites to come across your home on the web. Avoid spammy "link exchanges." Instead, make this happen through old-fashioned networking using today's tools. Study your colleagues' sites, then reach out via email or on social media. Attend live events, shake some hands, and talk to people. Show them you've done your research: explain what you enjoy on their sites and why you think their audience might benefit from your information. Expect to get no response from some, a straight out "no" from others ... and a few "yeses." Every single yes will help people find your site, so work hard for each one.

Don't Be Afraid to Fly by the Seat of Your Pants

After all these planning recommendations, you may think every future piece of content must fit rigidly within this content structure you've created. If that was the case, you'd miss out on the accidental hits you create when you listen to the audience you're building.

Here's the thing: if you follow this plan and consistently create content that fits within the categories you set up, eventually you'll attract real, live readers. And these real people — individuals, one and all — will have real problems and questions.

Your real live readers will be the richest, most inspiring source of ideas you'll find. Many of their questions and comments will inspire content that will fit right into the plan you've created.

But not all of it. And that's OK.

Use your categories as a loose guide to keep you on track. If you notice a certain topic has taken hold — getting lots of feedback, shares, and comments — consider adding it to your category list if you think it will continue to be popular.

Creating content that responds to the needs of your readers is smart. Most content creators I know work this way.

So listen to your audience. Write content that answers their most pressing questions. Use your categories as a loose guide to keep you on track.

Why You Should Build a Content Idea Library – Today

It's the content creator's version of a nightmare. You need to publish a new piece of content tomorrow. Meanwhile, your mind has gone completely blank, and sweat is beading on your upper lip. You stare at your screen, and that *cursed cursor* blinks back at you, unfeeling and cruel.

"What should I write about?"

In those panicky moments, we need all the support we can get. That's why I recommend you build a content idea library. A content idea library stores your overall site plans so you can take them out and review them at a moment's notice. It contains article ideas in an easy-to-skim format. A content idea library is a supportive source of inspiration and ideas for all your future content.

When you set it up right, your content idea library will help you avoid that sweaty upper lip scenario entirely. When it's time to write content, you can fire it up or flip it open, grab an idea, and start working on your content.

What a Content Idea Library Looks Like

In the previous section, we talked about how to create a content plan using categories and content ideas to guide your website's content.

A content idea library is the working space where your content plan lives. It contains these two main components:

Your overall category plan for reference. The category plan we came up with earlier provides a structure and a source of ideas for upcoming content. It should feature prominently in your content idea library so you keep your main categories at the top of your mind.

An easy place to drop new content ideas you'll have. As you become more proficient at content creation, you'll find inspiration all around you: in the questions readers ask, in your own developing opinions, in casual conversations with family and friends. The ideal content idea library will be easy to access and add ideas to in a moment's notice.

A truly perfect content idea library would also contain a running list of already-created content, like a content inventory that would update over time. This would help you find similar content topics so you could link between them. You could keep a list of any promotions associated with the content you've created. And you could use the inventory to ensure you're covering your content categories consistently, and not building up one category while you forget about another.

As far as I know, this "perfect" content inventory tool has yet to be created. But now you know my dream.

A Basic Blueprint for Your Content Idea Library

There are several ways you can hand-build a content idea library using tools you probably already have. The most important advice before you begin, though, is this:

> *The tools you use to create your content idea library aren't as important as this: build one content idea library only.*

Don't stash ideas in several places. Experiment with various systems if needed, then pick one and stick to it. I'm going to offer a digital solution and a tactile solution. Most people prefer one over the other. Think about whether you'll find a paper solution easier, or one that will involve your computer and/or phone.

Whether it's digital or tactile, your content idea library will contain these elements:

- One main page or section with your category plan so you can quickly reference it.
- Subsections for categories with places to add content ideas.
- A way to indicate which ideas you've used.
- A place to add notes about other content to link to, ideas you want to be sure to include, publication dates, and the like.

The digital content idea library

For many of us who've moved firmly over to the paperless world, noting content ideas on paper seems like a recipe for disaster. We're experts at misplacing paper, and we rely on searchable, editable, digital solutions for most of our work.

If that describes you, look for tools that will allow you to set up a structure like this. At the time of this writing, there were lots of digital tools available that would allow you to set up the structure above. You have to find the tool that works best for you — and I'm not just saying that! You're going to be using this content idea library for years. Find a system you enjoy using.

Spend some time upfront experimenting with a couple of different systems if you don't see a favorite below. Look for one that feels simple and easy to use, allows you to get in and out of it quickly, and makes you feel supported in your work. A few recommendations that are all available at the time of this writing:

Trello: The editorial team at Copyblogger uses a Trello board to track our content ideas. You can easily add images or links to documents, which would allow you to add your category plan for easy reference. Each category could have its own list, and you could add content ideas on cards. Trello cards can be assigned to individuals, and they carry a due date. You can quickly add content ideas, resources, and links you want to include right on the cards. Images and reference material can be stashed on content idea cards. Cards can be archived once content has been created. Trello is available on a computer, tablet, or phone.

Evernote: An Evernote notebook called "Content Idea Library" would be easy to access from any device. Inside the notebook, you could have one note with your category plan. You could have a separate note for each category you want to cover. Each category note would feature content ideas that fall under that category. As you create the content, you can add the links to this document for a record of what you've accomplished.

Spreadsheet: If you're drawn to spreadsheets, they could also work as pared-down content idea libraries. Use the first page to store your overall category plan. Then add a worksheet where you'll map out content categories. You can add rows as needed below each category so you can drop ideas into it. This solution is simple by design, but you can add features like due dates and status simply by adding columns to the spreadsheet.

Mind map: If you're a mind map fan like I am, you could set up your category plan in a mind map, and add content ideas as branches. This is another simple approach, but sometimes simpler systems are easier to sustain.

The tactile content idea library

Some people have a strong preference for writing ideas out by hand. If that sounds like you, try these methods for building a content idea library you can add to over time.

Keep a notebook: The perfect notebook for your content idea library is one that's portable and has enough room to expand. Ideally, you'll keep this nearby as you go through your day: content ideas can hit you when you least expect them. Sketch out your category plan at the front of your notebook. Add category names to the tops of pages, then leave room to write down content ideas and notes. Cross ideas off as you create them.

Use index cards: If you're struggling to find the balance between portability and having room to grow, index cards might be the solution. Use colored cards for your content categories and white cards for your content ideas. Keep a few cards with you wherever you are so you can jot down ideas when they strike you, then simply file them away in the correct category when you can.

How Content Categories Build Authority

When we open a restaurant menu that has too many unrelated types of dishes, we assume it's a "jack of all trades, master of none" situation and don't have high expectations for the quality of the food.

The same can be said of our websites. If we try to be all things to all people, our authority gets diluted, and so does our brand. But when we limit our categories and develop deep content resources on in-demand topics, we get the traction we need to build authority and an audience who trusts us to deliver high-quality solutions, both free and paid.

How to Plan Your Content: A Checklist

Use the checklist below to plan the content you'll create:

☐ **Build a category plan to guide you.** Think about your readers and what they'll want to understand and master within your larger topic.

☐ **Aim for eight to ten categories total.** If you're just starting out, choose four or five essential categories, so you have room to expand over time.

☐ **Use language your audience uses.** Avoid jargon and aim for clarity in your category names and in all your written content.

☐ **Create a content idea library.** Choose one place to store your ideas. Include your category plan so you can keep your overall structure at the top of your mind. Use a tool you'll enjoy adding ideas to over time.

CHAPTER 4

Matching Your Content to Your Customer's Journey

Prospects and customers go through a process of getting to know your business until they feel comfortable opening their wallets and doing business with you.

It's called a "customer journey." Although many have tried to map it out and identify key steps along the way, the reality is that the journey taken will look a little different for each person.

Customer journeys are as different as the people who take them.

Content marketing is designed to facilitate this journey — no matter what it looks like — by offering up the right information every step of the way.

I want to share a way of thinking about the customer journey that the Copyblogger editorial team has developed as we work together to produce the Copyblogger blog.

We took a step back and looked at how we could best serve our entire audience: the ones who were just finding Copyblogger *and* the ones who'd been reading for years. We developed a technique for classifying the content we create, and it has been enormously helpful in guiding our topic choices and developing an editorial calendar that meets the needs of the people who come to our site.

This classification system will ensure that you deliver the content your prospects need to understand your topic, develop trust in your business, and feel comfortable entering into a business relationship.

Identify and Write to Your Customer's Experience Level

The editorial team identified three labels we use to pinpoint who we're writing for when we create specific content on our site. Pay close attention to the questions associated with each label. That's where the magic happens!

Beginner, or What is ___?

Your beginning readers comprise a vast audience, and it's important to serve them well.

I've seen it many times: a content creator picks a topic and begins writing about it consistently over time. Researching, writing, and teaching a topic inevitably leads to a more in-depth understanding of it. As their knowledge deepens, their content becomes richer. But they "forget" what beginners want and need.

This is a mistake. Many of your prospects will find your site because they do a web search for something they'd like to know. They find your content because it answers their question. And they stick around because they see that your information is consistently helpful.

These beginning readers are ripe prospects who you can move along a customer journey using your content. To write content that helps them, think about your main topic and all the related subtopics. Here's an example:

You write about learning to run for an audience of readers who've never run before. Many of the people who come to your site will be complete beginners — people who need to know the basics. They're asking . . .

Post ideas to answer the What is ___? Question:

- What could running do for me?
- Do I have to run fast to be considered a runner?
- What is the difference between a regular sneaker and a running shoe?
- Why is proper training necessary?
- What is a realistic schedule I can use to go from no activity to running a 5k race?

- What are warm ups, cool downs, and sprints, and why should I do them?

Beginners have questions — lots of them. And some of them are so basic they might be embarrassed to ask them if they were standing right in front of you. Guess what? That's why they're doing a web search!

So make sure you provide plenty of content that answers the "What is ____?" fundamental questions that are running through your beginning readers' minds.

Intermediate, or How Do I Do ___?

Your intermediate readers have gone beyond the basics. They've found answers to their "embarrassing" questions. Now they're working to achieve mastery. They have a vision, they're working toward it, and they're looking to your content for help.

Intermediate readers are voracious consumers of "how-to" style content. They want tips, checklists, "ultimate guides" and step-by-step tutorials. And when you deliver this kind of content to them, they'll save it, re-visit it, and share it with their friends because they found it useful.

Let's take another look at our website about helping non-runners learn to run. They're asking …

Post ideas to answer the How do I do ___? question:

- What kind of shoe offers the best support for running hills?
- How can I find running buddies in my community?
- What should I do about dogs that approach me while I'm running?
- What are the best apps for mapping my run?
- How can I stay hydrated when I run in the heat?
- What's the best way to control my body temperature when running in the cold?

Advanced, or How Do I Get Better at ___?

Advanced readers have the basics down pat. They've also mastered intermediate-level questions and know "how to" do most activities and tasks associated with your topic.

When they get to this point, they morph into advanced readers. And they're still looking to you and your content to guide them on their journeys. After all, you're the authoritative voice who got them to this point, right? Your site is their preferred place to learn.

Advanced readers want to improve their performance. They know how to do the basics. Now they want to get better, faster, and more efficient.
They're asking …

Post ideas to answer the How do I get better at ___? question:

- How can I increase my stamina so I can run longer distances?
- What's a good strategy for winning a 5k race?
- How can I keep running even in my 60s, 70s, 80s, and beyond?
- What's a reliable training regimen to increase speed?
- How can I adopt a winning mindset on race day?
- Where can I find safe and fun running routes while traveling?

What Percentage of Your Content Should You Write for Each Group?

Oh, I'd love to give you a formula here. I really would! But this is something you're going to have to figure out for your own website and audience. A few guidelines:

Write mostly for beginners. The beginner audience is massive, and reaching out to them will help you bring in a steady stream of prospects who will be forever grateful you were there for them when they were asking their newbie questions.

Listen carefully, and note what people are asking about. If you notice lots of comments on your site or on social media platforms that feature intermediate and advanced questions, write content to answer those.

Notice objections and write answers to them. Any time you make an offer, people will find all sorts of reasons *not to buy.* When you're writing a sales page, for example, you'll want to be sure you're answering those objections and providing reassurance in your copy.

But your regular content can answer objections, too. As a matter of fact, using content this way makes it much easier to sell something once you're ready because you've responded to questions and met objections slowly and naturally with the information you've shared over time.

Using our example above, a few objections — and the content that will answer them — might be:

Objection: I'll never be a runner: I'm too out of shape.
Content: *5 Inspiring Examples of Great Runners Who Don't Look Like Typical Athletes*

Objection: I don't have time to run.
Content: *A Simple Way to Run Daily and Still Have All the Time You Need*

Objection: Others can run but I've tried, and I know I can't do it.
Content: *3 Surefire Ways to Ease Into Becoming a Runner — Even if You've Failed Before*

This approach to content — thinking in terms of beginner, intermediate, and advanced — will influence the topics you cover and how you deliver your information.

Matching Your Content to Your Customer's Journey: A Checklist

☐ **Serve up content for every step of your prospect's journey.** Make sure you have plenty of content for beginners and ample content for those who are at an intermediate or advanced level.

☐ **For beginning readers, answer What is ___?** Beginning content defines a topic and helps web searchers expand their understanding of the basics.

☐ **For intermediate readers, answer How Do I Do ___?** Intermediate readers want to know how to apply what they're learning to their lives and situations. "How-to" content fits perfectly into this category.

☐ **For advanced readers, answer How Do I Get Better at ___?** Advanced readers crave mastery. What content can you create that will help them get really good at your topic?

The "Lazy" (Efficient) Approach to Content Creation

CHAPTER 5

The 7-Part Formula for Content Creation, an Introduction

There I was back in early 2010, betting the farm on content marketing. I had just started the Big Brand System website and was staring at the abyss of my very empty blog that I was scrambling to write weekly posts for.

My content "plan" consisted of a series of ten posts I called Design 101. The posts outlined design basics that anyone who wants to build a recognizable brand needs to understand. Design 101 was like my design manifesto: it contained the concepts I wished my clients understood during all those years I was showing them my work.

I later repurposed Design 101 into a series of email messages and used this "mini course" as an enticement to invite people to join my email list.

Smart plan, those initial posts. Right?

It was, actually. It served me well. For the first ten weeks.

After that, I was confronted by that moment we all must face:

Oh no! What should I write about now?

Of course, that moment never really goes away. It repeats itself on a regular basis for most of us, and we get used to it. The good news is that when you've created a content idea library — a reliable, easy-to-use place to maintain your content plan and ideas — you'll always have a source to draw from. And when you get into the habit of listening closely to the concerns of your audience, you'll find new inspiration in your interactions with them.

The Moment of Truth: Time to Write Your Content

Let's say you need to write a piece of content for your website. You know what you want to write about. Now what?

That's what we'll talk about in the chapters ahead. Coming up, I'm going to share the part of this book that I'm hoping you'll use as a reference guide whenever you need to create content.

My dream is that this book will be a "desktop companion" for you. I am hoping you'll find a way to keep the information in the next seven chapters close at hand so it can be there to guide you as you put your content together.

And "put your content together" is a deliberate choice of words!

Content marketing can be daunting. But the approach I'll show you starting in this chapter should help to make creating content much, much easier.

We're going to split a piece of content into its component parts. I'll give you guidance, tips, and hints for each one separately.

I believe that it's much easier to tackle a big task when you break it down into smaller pieces and work on one piece at a time. That's what we're going to do with the content creation process.

What's especially tough about content marketing is that so many of us who find ourselves creating it don't *really* consider ourselves born writers.

I know I didn't. Here I was building an online presence based on content marketing, and I had no writing training at all. I hadn't done it professionally ever.

What was I thinking?

But sometimes the best results happen when you forge ahead and learn as you go. It might be nerve-wracking because you're learning publicly — others can see your first feeble attempts. But there aren't that many people paying attention at first. You can learn in a relatively private environment. More people will find your site after some time passes, and when they do, your writing will have improved.

Breaking Content Down to Build It Up

Once I wrote the last word of my Design 101 series, my real content marketing job began. I was in the middle of taking an online course and I found the courage to announce my new site inside the course forum. Some of my first website comments came from fellow students in that course. In their comments and questions, I found inspiration for future posts.

Designers are trained to see and respond to patterns. We look at lines of type and group them together and align them. We see repeating colors and arrange them on the page in a way that emphasizes the pattern and draws your eyes to it.

I guess that's why I noticed a pattern to the content I was creating.

The more I wrote, the more I saw that all great content consisted of the same seven components. And over time, I saw that when a piece of content was successful — when it generated traffic, inspired comments, and was widely shared — every single one of these seven components was doing its job well.

I started thinking about these content elements as separate entities that were fulfilling specific roles inside my content.

I focused my efforts on learning to master the writing of each separate component of a piece of content. They all had their own set of rules and best practices, so it wasn't an easy task. But I found that as I absorbed and integrated these best practices into my writing, my content got stronger. It became easier to read. It inspired more comments — sometimes passionately opinionated ones! And most importantly, it began to build my business, grow my email list, and send me more prospects and customers for my online business.

To my great delight, I found that thinking about content like this also made it seem much less daunting to create. It started to feel like a seven-step recipe for content creation: as long as I remembered how to do each step, the end result would be a delicious, nutritious, and cohesive content "meal" that would attract the right readers and motivate them to act.

The other delightful surprise was that writing content became faster — the same way cooking a new, strange recipe becomes faster after you've gone through the steps a few times. Eventually, you might even be able to set the recipe aside and just focus on enjoying the process of cooking.

Let's look at the seven components now. In the chapters ahead, we'll tackle each one separately. You'll be able to use each of the seven chapters to guide you as you learn to master these elements of successful content.

Seven Essential Elements of Successful Content

Content marketing works best when every one of the elements below are present, well-written, and irresistible. Each one needs to be polished so it pulls its weight and does its job in your article.

1. The compelling headline: Want your content to be read? Spend lots and *lots* of time (way more than you think) working to write an engaging headline. In this chapter, we'll define "compelling" as it applies to headlines. I'll share tips for writing headlines that get clicks. You'll get some headline formulas you can use when you're stuck. And I'll recommend a headline habit that you can adopt to make writing great headlines easier and faster.

2. The first sentence: I know, I know … a whole chapter about one sentence? Really? It may sound crazy, but the very first sentence of your article is a make-or-break moment. It's important to get it right, because if you don't, readers will click away and look elsewhere for their information. This chapter will share specific tips for writing the kind of first sentence that grabs readers, draws them in, and keeps them reading the rest of your content.

3. The intro section: You may have never realized that all content has an intro section, but it does. Just like most homes have a front porch or an entry area just inside the front door, your content has an intro section that serves as a transition to your main content section. Its job is incredibly important. This is the first place on the page where you're asking the reader to commit to reading what you've written. They've seen your headline and clicked on it. They've read your first sentence. Now you're asking them to *keep reading*. This chapter will show you how to motivate readers to make that commitment to your page with simple tips and guidance you can apply immediately.

4. The subheads: If you're not currently using subheads, you will be once you read this chapter! Subheads are one of the most important ways you can make your online content easier to digest. In this chapter, we'll cover the "dual readership path" and how you can use it to your advantage. You'll get tips and guidance for writing subheads that keep readers absorbed, so they continue reading all the way through your article.

5. The main copy: What's "the main copy?" It's *everything else*. It's all the writing you're going to do outside of the sections above and the sections below. It's the meat of your content — the heart of your post. With the tips in this chapter, you'll discover best practices for making the heart of your post easy to read, visually interesting, and faster to put together.

6. The summary: Here's another content section you may not have noticed before, but all good posts feature it. At some point toward the end of your content, you need to wrap up the topic you're covering and move readers to the final content element — the call to action. The summary section does this for your readers. When you put it together with the tips I'll share, your summary will create a smooth transition from sharing useful information to asking your reader to do something with what they've just learned.

7. The call to action: Content marketing serves a business purpose. It helps your website get found, it attracts prospects to your business, and it gives you a way to develop a trust-based relationship with them. But if you don't ask your readers to take action, you might as well skip the whole exercise! Writing effective calls to action may not come naturally to you now, but by the time you finish this chapter, you'll feel more confident about creating them. You'll have a guide to help you put together calls to action that motivate readers to do something once they've finished reading.

How to Use the Next Seven Chapters

If you've bought and are holding a physical copy of this book (thank you), I give you my wholehearted permission to deface it at this point. As mentioned, I want these next seven chapters to serve as a guide as you create your content in the future.

So go ahead and fold down the corner of the first page of each of the next seven chapters. Give those chapter pages dog-eared corners to make them easier to find! Or grab some sticky notes and place one at the beginning of each of the next seven chapters to make them easier to flip to.

If you're reading on an electronic device, I recommend you use the bookmarking feature to add a marker at the beginning of each of the next chapters. This will create your own private table of contents that you can use to go directly to the chapter you need most.

And if you're listening to this on audio, most audio players have a way to bookmark, too! It took me months to realize this, so I want to share it with you in case you haven't found it. The exact technique for creating a bookmark will vary by player, but poke around on yours and do some experimenting until you find how to create an easily searchable bookmark in your audio device.

*The main thing I want you to do is make these next seven chapters easy to find
and use in the future.*

Permission to Write Out of Order Granted

Here's something else to keep in mind. You don't have to write your content from
top to bottom. If you have a piece of content planned, and you think of the subheads
before the headline, that's perfectly fine. If you write the call to action first and the first
sentence last, that's OK, too.

This has happened to me many times. An idea for a section of my content strikes
me — sometimes it's the first sentence; or the subheads; or the call to action. It doesn't
matter if you write out of order. Approach your content as components of a whole and
you can work on the section you feel most inspired to write.

If you're just starting out with content creation, though, you may find it easier to
write your headline and subheads first. I call these the "backbone" of your article because
they provide a beautiful structure you can hang the rest of your words on. I'll share more
on this idea later in this book.

Use the next seven chapters however you need: flip to the section you're working on,
no matter what order you need it.

Once you start thinking about your content in this "component" way, you may find
yourself getting stuck on a specific element. The element that trips you up could vary
from one piece of content to another, so I want you to be able to dive into this book and
find the help you need when you need it.

Don't Preach: Write to One Reader

Creating content can be nerve-wracking because your words are going to be out in
public where anyone can read them. Knowing that dozens, hundreds, and maybe thousands of people will read what you wrote might cause you to write like you're addressing
a large crowd. Don't.

Keep in mind that you should always write to one single person. It doesn't matter if
hundreds or thousands of people may read your words: write like it's *just the two of you*
— because it is.

At any given moment, it's truly just the two of you — you the author, and your individual reader. Your reader is a person you're reaching out to with information and encouragement. *Write to this one person.* Your writing will sound more natural, approachable, and friendly.

Ready? Let's tackle headlines first.

Get Free Content Strategy Tools When You Register

When you register for the free content marketing resources I've created for you, you'll get extra help as you apply the information in these chapters to your own content strategy. Go to MasterContentMarketing.com/bonus and sign up!

CHAPTER 6

1. Headline:
Start with a Bang That Gets Attention

A headline can do more than simply grab attention. A great headline can also communicate a full message to its intended audience, and it absolutely must lure the reader into your body text. – Brian Clark

Your headline is where the relationship with your reader begins. That's why it's important to start with a bang so you can attract the reader you want to reach, and motivate them to continue reading.

Your headline is like those chalkboard signs on the sidewalk in front of a store or restaurant.

You've seen those, right? They're placed smack in the middle of high-traffic walkways. The best chalkboard signs make a promise and create curiosity. *They make you want to step inside the business.*

Using content to market your business is smart. But it only works if people find your content and "step inside it" so they can read it and take action.

The best headlines do this — they make people want to read your content. They get them past their state of inertia by creating curiosity and making a promise. They make the all-important click happen.

Once inside, it's up to the business to meet and exceed the expectations set by the chalkboard sign that got them there.

That's why it's important to feel comfortable adopting a slightly more "sales-y" tone in your headline than what you'll use in the rest of your content. Your headline needs to "sell" your content so it gets read.

I know you want your content to be helpful, useful, and approachable. We all do. But if you work hard to make it all those things and no one reads it, what's the point?

Think of your headline like an *advocate* for your content. It's out there in the high-traffic environment of the web advocating for the amazing information you've created. *It's selling it, baby.* And that's OK!

Don't be afraid to write a headline that "sells" your content. That's the #1 job of any headline. If your headline fails, so will the rest of your content.

Here's what you need to remember: as long as your content is consistently excellent, you should feel no shame giving it the best possible chance to be discovered by taking the time to write headlines that make people want to click.

And this book is all about helping you create consistently excellent content. By the time you finish reading, you'll have mastered how to do that. You'll *want* people to read what you've worked so hard to create.

So for now, let's work on that headline. Because your content is going to be amazing, and I want people to find it! I know you do, too.

Don't Be Shy: How to Create Headlines That Get Clicks

There are two things I'm going to recommend you put into place so you can master the art of writing headlines. One is a *practice* you can adopt, and the other is a *group of tools* I'd like you to keep at hand.

Make no mistake: this particular content element is one of the most important of the seven we'll cover. So even though it's only one of seven, please plan to spend extra effort on mastering the art of writing compelling headlines. A lot of your content's success depends on them.

The moment someone sees your headline, the fate of your content is being decided — people will either click through to read what you wrote, or they won't.

Practice Makes Perfect: How to Become a Headline Machine

There's a ritual I go through every time I create a piece of content. It happens at the beginning of the process. I turn a switch, and I become a *headline machine.*

Let me tell you what this looks like.

I know what I want to write about. I open the thesaurus on my computer. I keep my headline inspiration files at hand (more on these in a moment). Then I begin writing headline ideas. Lots of them.

Where do I do that writing? For me, headline writing happens in a simple text document. I have my text document open in front of me, and I turn on my headline creation spigot.

OK, I don't *really* have a spigot. But it feels like it sometimes. The headline ideas start to drip out. Sometimes they come out painfully slowly. Sometimes they come in a rush — almost faster than I can type.

If headline ideas aren't flowing as fast as you'd like them to, don't fret — just stay at the ready, pen and paper in hand or fingers on your keyboard.

The first headlines on the list are usually pretty boring. They're often quite clichéd. Most won't work at all, and that's OK — at this point in the process, you're just trying to get ideas on paper. Sometimes you have to "unplug" your brain and get the dumb ideas out first so the great ideas (which are back there, but hiding) can come to the forefront.

Sometimes a headline won't work in its entirety, but a piece of it will. Just keep writing — don't judge. You want to deliver as many ideas as you can into your document so that you have "ingredients" to work with. Don't pressure yourself to achieve perfection.

At this stage in my own process, I write, and write, and write headlines. How many? At *least* a dozen. Sometimes many, many more: 40 or 50. Some days, it takes that many tries until you hit on one that truly works.

How do you know you've hit on a headline idea that works?

You feel it in your gut. A good headline has the effect of *making you want to write the content.* I can't tell you how many times this has happened to me! When you write a great headline, you get excited about the content approach you'll take and the information you'll share. A good headline makes you want to create content that lives up to its potential.

It makes a big, bold promise. Your headline is asking people to commit their time and energy to reading your content. They need to know they'll get something from the effort they'll expend. Make them a promise they can't refuse.

It creates curiosity. The best headlines make a big promise … but they don't deliver on that promise. *The delivery happens in the content itself.* That's why "3 Simple Strategies to Earn Your New Kitten's Unending Devotion" will always get more clicks than "Make Your New Kitten Love You with Good Food, Fresh Water, and a Clean Litter Box."

The first step in mastering headlines is to become a headline creation machine every time you want to write a piece of content. Plan to devote significant time and energy to this task. It's extremely important that you give your content the best possible opportunity in this world by giving it a headline that sells the benefits your content is going to deliver.

The tools you'll use to craft headlines that work are what we'll talk about next.

Your Headline Creation Tools

It's always easier to go straight into creation mode when you have a reliable set of tools and you take them out and have them close by. Doing this — deciding on your favorite tools and then placing them in front of you before you begin working — will serve as a trigger to tell your brain it's time to get in gear.

Your "blank sheet of paper." A blank sheet of paper nowadays is most often a blank text document on a computer. I'm often asked what I use, and you know what? It doesn't matter one bit what works for me. We're talking about you here! And the best tool for you is the one you're most comfortable using to write. It's the one that you feel the least resistance about using. You don't need anything fancy: paper and a pencil, or a simple text editor or word processor will work fine.

Your headline inspiration sources. When it comes to headlines, there's nothing new under the sun. There are certain headline formulas that human beings respond to consistently, so there's no need to invent your headline completely from scratch. Keep some models in front of you to inspire your thinking and generate ideas faster. And don't worry that you'll be "copying" someone else's work.

I look at it like painting: give two people the same paintbrush and the same three colors of paint, and I guarantee the art they create will be different.

So arm yourself with some headline inspiration to get a head start. Toward the end of this chapter, you'll find ideas and formulas you can try.

I encourage you to use more than one source for headline inspiration. The web is full of headline resources, and many are free.

There are two I always keep at hand. The first is Rainmaker Digital's Magnetic Headlines ebook, which is free in exchange for a site registration at copyblogger.com/magnetic-headlines. The second is *Headline Hacks*, by Jon Morrow of Smart Blogger, which is also free in exchange for an email address at smartblogger.com/headline-hacks.

An easy-to-use thesaurus. Once in headline writing mode, you'll be pumping out ideas quickly, and you might find yourself getting stuck on certain boring words that aren't generating the sense of anticipation and excitement you want your headline to create. My favorite way around this is to have a thesaurus close by. My personal preference is the one that's built into my computer's operating system, but you can use an online thesaurus, too. Paper thesauruses also work, but I prefer digital versions because results are clickable hyperlinks you can follow to find even more options. I have found many a unique word by following the rabbit trail of links a few levels deep in my digital thesaurus.

(Optional) A timer. For an easy way to boost your motivation, try setting a goal for a certain number of headlines in a limited amount of time. Set your timer for 10 minutes, and come up with 20 headlines. Or give yourself five minutes to come up with ten.

Get Inside Your Reader's Head to Write Headlines That Get Clicks

Let's be ultra-literal about the word "headline" just for a moment.

The best headlines tap into lines of thinking that are already going through your reader's head. Head. Lines.

What *are* those lines of thinking? How do you know what your reader is thinking?

Once you've gathered an audience, this is much easier because your readers will tell you, either explicitly or implicitly.

Explicit feedback happens in the form of comments, replies to emails, posts on forums you may host, or messages and comments on social media platforms. Explicit feedback happens when your customers speak directly to you, using their own words and vocabulary to communicate their thoughts, feelings, and questions.

Implicit feedback happens in the form of actions taken in response to your content. This includes things like social shares; the total number of comments and re-tweets; the open rate on an email message; the growth of your email list; or the number of sales made from an offer inside your content.

It's important to pay attention to both types of feedback, but pay close attention to explicit feedback. Explicit feedback is gold!

Mine your explicit feedback — where your prospects and customers are using their own words to communicate with you — and note how your prospects and customers talk about their challenges. Find the exact words and phrases they use to describe their situation, and use those in your content marketing — especially in your headlines.

Eugene Schwartz, in his classic book, *Breakthrough Advertising,* talks about channeling mass desire toward your product. In this example, your product is the piece of content you want people to read.

What does "channeling mass desire" mean, and how can you use it to write better headlines?

To paraphrase Schwartz's recommendations and apply them to headline writing:

- Identify the most compelling desire around your content topic.
- Mention the desire in your headline, and promise a way to satisfy it.

Did you ever take a psychology class? If so, you'll remember Maslow's Hierarchy of Needs. Abraham Maslow categorized the needs every human shares into:

- Physiological needs like food and water
- Security needs like a safe place to live
- Emotional needs like love and friendship
- Esteem needs like self-confidence and the respect of others

The categories above need to be met before we can meet higher-level needs like self-actualization through personal creativity, morality, and our ability to solve problems.

When your headline identifies the basic needs and desires readers have around the topic you're writing about, you'll tap into powerful psychological drivers that will help move them to click on your headline and read your content.

And what about those headline formulas? They're coming after the next section, as promised. First, we need to have a chat about keywords.

Are Keywords Important?

Keywords and *keyword phrases* refer to the words people type into search engines when they're looking for something on the web.

With so many sites online now, you're smart to aim for keyword phrases rather than single keywords. People have learned to search by typing in full questions or multi-word phrases — their results are more targeted and useful when they do.

It's important to spend some time familiarizing yourself with the phrases your readers might type into a search box. We've already covered some simple ways to find out the natural language people are using:

- Read your site's comments and pick up language from there.
- Pay close attention to the words used to talk about your topic on social media.
- Read and respond to anyone who replies to emails you send (and note the language they use and the questions they ask).

Other ways to familiarize yourself with keywords:

- For a quick technique, try typing the beginnings of the words *you* think people will use into a Google search bar and watch the suggested topics that appear.
- Google offers a "keyword planner" as part of their AdWords campaign tools. You need to have a Google account to use this. It can be a bit confusing at first, but do a quick search and you'll find plenty of tips.
- Some website software, including the Rainmaker Platform made by the company I work for, will show you the phrases people typed into a search engine that led them to your site.

Writing content that uses the exact words searchers are typing can help your content get found. In the end, though, it's important that your headline be compelling — that it *sell* the content you're about to share.

So incorporate keyword phrases in your headline *where they can be used naturally*. If your headline sounds stilted or unnatural when you add your keyword phrase, leave it out. Instead, try using the phrase in a subhead and elsewhere in your content to help it get found.

The main point here is to *use the words your audience uses*. As you get to know your audience, you'll speak their language intuitively. But at the beginning, do keyword research.

Remember in the previous chapter how I recommended you add a sticky note, bookmark, or dog-eared corner to each of these seven chapters? You might want to add an extra one to the section that follows: I'm about to share winning headline formulas you'll want to refer to frequently as you prepare to churn out headline ideas for your future content.

Plug Into These All-Time Winning Headline Formulas

In this section, you'll find formulas you can try when you're in headline-writing mode. Wherever a number would go, I've used an "X." And where a topic-specific word would go, I've inserted a _____ so you can fill in a word that works for your topic. In some cases, a specific kind of information should be in the blank: if so, I've put it between brackets.

Current recommendations for headline length hover around 70 characters total. If you go beyond 70 characters, your headline may get cut off in search engine results.

For this reason, it's important to try to put the most compelling words toward the front of your headline rather than at the end. If there's any chance the end is going to be cut off, you want to be sure that whatever is cut doesn't detract from the meaning and impact of your headline.

As you try plugging the topic you want to write about into the headline formulas below, remember this: great headlines are a combination of formulas plus an intimate understanding of the hopes, dreams, fears, and challenges of the people you want to reach. So don't just drop words in below and call it a day. Keep your readers at the front of your mind so you can write headlines that will resonate with their needs.

And one more thing — you want to create curiosity but not thoroughly confuse. There's a delicate balance.

Remember ABC: Always Be Clear. Your reader should understand what your headline says without a doubt. Any curiosity you create should be about the content they'll read, not about the meaning of your headline.

Read on for fifty headline formulas that will work hard to sell the great content you'll create.

How-to Headlines

Why they work:
- They promise a result
- They empower the reader

Examples:
- How to Master _____ in X Simple Steps
- How to [Achieve This Desirable Result] in Less Than X Minutes a Day
- How to [Do This Bold Thing], [Do This Other Bold Thing], and [Get This Bold Result]
- How to Make Fast, Easy [Something that is Normally Tedious to Do]
- How to Get [This Big Result] from [This Unexpected Ingredient or Action]

List or Number Headlines

Why they work:
- They're specific
- They promise digestible information (make the main points into subheads and number them so they're easy to follow)

Examples:
- X Surprising Tips That Will Transform Your Approach to ____
- X Secrets That Professional ____ Don't Want You to Know
- X Simple Ways to Get [This Attractive Result]
- X Ways to Multiply Your ____ Results in Just X Days
- X Extraordinary ____ That Will Transform Your [Problem or Challenge]

Colon Headlines

Why they work:
- They fit two approaches into one headline: factual and emotional
- They allow you to list your keyword at the front and enticing information toward the end

Examples:
- [Content Topic]: The Only Guide You'll Ever Need
- [Content Topic]: An Alternative Approach That Really Works
- [Content Topic]: How to [Get This Result] on a Tiny Budget
- [Content Topic]: What the Pros Don't Want You to Know
- [Content Topic]: X Simple Ways to [Get This Result] [In X Time]

Unexpected Word Headlines

Why they work:
- They create curiosity and make your reader want to know more
- They can be written with your thesaurus in hand, so they're easy to generate

Examples:
- X Peculiar Approaches to [Your Topic] That Make Perfect Sense
- Why These X Grim Realities About [Your Topic] Should Surprise and Delight You
- [Your Topic]: X Splendid Solutions for [Challenge] You'll Want to Try Today
- X Ways to Instantly Vaporize Your Fears About [Your Topic]
- How So Many Disheartened [Your Audience] Finally Achieve [A Big Goal Your Audience Has]

What or Why Headlines

Why they work:
- They promise an easy-to-understand explanation
- They offer straightforward information that meets searchers' needs

Examples:

- Why Mastering [Your Topic] is Essential in [Current Year]
- What Powerful [Advanced Audience Members] Know That You Don't
- Why You Should Never [Do This] When Starting Out with [Your Topic]
- What You Can Learn from [Unexpected Source of Inspiration] to Help You Build a Better [Topic]
- Why [Unexpected Technique] is the Fastest Way to Win at [Your Topic]

Announcement Headlines

Why they work:

- They grab attention the way breaking news does
- They promise to share something new, exciting, exclusive

Examples:

- Introducing a Tested Solution to [Sticky Problem Your Audience Suffers]
- New! A [Descriptive Word + Product] at a Low Introductory Price
- It's Here: The Ultimate Guide to Mastering [Your Topic]
- Announcing a Better Approach to Getting the [Meaningful Result] You've Always Wanted
- Just Released: The All-in-One Solution to Solving [Sticky Problem] Once and For All

Transformation Headlines

Why they work:

- They promise to take the reader from point A to point B
- The reader expects an interesting story and wants to find out more

Examples:

- How I Went from Failing at [Topic] to Earning [X] as a [Topic] Expert
- From [Uninteresting Career] to [Desirable Career]: One Woman's Riveting Journey
- Finally! Go From [Undesirable State] to [Desirable State] in X Simple Steps
- You Too Can Become [Desirable Result] Even If You're Starting from [Undesirable State]

- X Outrageously Simple Ways to Take [Undesirable State] and Turn It Into [Desirable State]

Question Headlines

Why they work:
- They appeal to beginners, who might have these exact questions running through their heads
- They appeal to people who are looking for the definitive answer to a question

Examples:
- What is [Your Topic]?
- Are You Ready for the Changing [Your Topic] Environment?
- How Often Should You [Maintenance Task Related to Your Topic]?
- Should You Pay Attention to [Breaking News About Your Topic]?
- Is Your [Topic] Broken? (Here's How to Fix It)

Analogy Headlines

Why they work:
- Used sparingly and carefully, they can surprise and delight your readers
- They promise a post that's light and easy to read

Examples:
- X Things [Unexpected Inspiration] Can Teach You About Mastering [Your Topic]
- What [Someone From History] Understood About [Your Topic]: X Inspiring Quotes
- How to Meet the [Challenge Around Topic] Like [an Animal or Someone from History]
- Why [Achieving Something Around Your Topic] is Like [a Favorite Holiday or Award]
- The [Famous Person or Event] Guide to [Accomplishing Something Topic-Related]

Combination Headlines

Why they work:
- They combine attention-grabbing elements from the formulas above with unexpected (and interesting) results
- They give you plenty of room to share compelling ideas

Examples:
- Free! A Revolutionary Approach to [Your Topic]: Details Inside
- Why Becoming a [Future State] Will Be the Hardest and Best Thing You Do
- How to Eliminate [Undesirable Outcome]: X Remarkably Easy Tips
- Why These X Powerful Moves Will Transform You into [Desirable State]
- It's Here! These X Absurdly Simple Changes Will [Transformation]

There you have it: fifty ideas you can use as starting points to get your headline machine into high gear. Keep the reader you want to reach in the front of your mind and plug in topic-specific nouns and verbs that will resonate with them.

Have fun with this, and remember: your headline is selling your content! Don't be afraid to grab attention with bold, attention-getting statements.

Headline: A Checklist

☐ **Don't be shy.** Your headline has an important job to do. It needs to pull readers out of their sleepy web-searcher state of mind and engage them in your content. Don't be afraid to take a slightly more "sales-y" approach for your headlines.

☐ **Practice makes perfect.** Plan to spend some time as a "headline machine," churning out many headline ideas until you have one that really works.

☐ **Keep your headline tools close by.** These include your blank sheet of paper (or blank document), a thesaurus, and your headline inspiration ideas. Optional: give yourself extra motivation to get your ideas down quickly by using a timer.

☐ **Use words your readers already use.** Avoid jargon or cleverness in headlines. Aim for clarity and use words your readers already use to describe their challenges.

☐ **Research keyword phrases, but don't feel obligated to use them.** It's more important that your headline "sell" your content: if a keyword phrase fits and sounds compelling, use it. If not, focus on crafting a headline that will get clicks and use the keyword phrases in a subhead or the content itself.

CHAPTER 7

2. First Sentence: Draw Readers Into Your Content

An opening line should invite the reader to begin the story. It should say: Listen. Come in here. You want to know about this. – Stephen King

I haven't seen much written about the most hard-working sentence of your content, much less an entire chapter devoted to it. I believe it's important to look at it as a separate element from the rest of your content and not lump it into the main content itself. That's why this short chapter will be devoted entirely to this one crucial sentence.

Here's the most important thing to remember about the first line of your piece of content:

The job of your first sentence is to help the reader make the transition from your headline into your introduction — and to keep them reading.

They've read your headline, and they've clicked. But their hand might still be hovering over that Back button. A compelling first sentence will keep them on the page.

How to Write a First Sentence That Makes Your Reader Yearn for More

There are a few tried-and-true approaches for writing compelling first sentences, and in this chapter, we'll examine them so you can try them yourself. I'll include examples of each approach, too.

Certain approaches may feel more comfortable for you: if you're a natural storyteller, opening with a story might seem appealing. And if you enjoy writing copy that captures attention, the "pitch"-style opening sentence might seem easy and fun to write.

My recommendation is that you start by using whichever first sentence style feels easiest to write.

Simply focusing on writing an especially compelling first sentence — no matter the style — will help create a more effective opening to your article. Most writers don't pay that much attention to this one sentence in their piece — you will, so yours will be better.

Once you've mastered the style that comes most naturally to you, move on to exploring some of the other types.

It's important to offer varied content to our readers: we don't want every article we write to open the same, predictable way.

Remember Picasso? Once he mastered an artistic style, he pushed himself to try (and eventually master) another style. That's one of the reasons we're still talking about him today — and it's how he became so proficient at so many different types of art.

So pick a style below and use it more than once. Use the example sentences below to discover how to structure an opening sentence using each style. Make the most of the impact you can have with that style and move on to mastering the next one.

Note: all "facts" in the examples that follow are completely made up.
That's why they're so shocking!

The Storyteller's Opening Sentence

If you're a born storyteller, this opening sentence style will feel very natural to you. The goal with this style of sentence is to draw the reader into a story — one that's *already in progress.*

Imagine there's something fascinating happening inside a room behind a closed door. You and the reader are standing in the darkened halfway outside and you crack open the door to get a glimpse of the action inside the room.

Of course, if this were a movie script, at the exact moment you open the door, someone will say something absolutely riveting, or someone will do something that leaves your mouth agape with surprise. That's how you keep people watching the action: you draw them in at a point of high interest.

Examples:

Madeline stood on the scale — palms sweaty and dreading the result — only to stare in shock at the number that appeared on the display.

Late on a Tuesday afternoon in April, they booted me out of their investor's club because they realized I was onto their dishonest schemes.

Patrick grabbed the arm of his new acquaintance and fired up his mobile phone: his business had a website he was proud of, and he couldn't wait to show it off.

Storyteller opening sentences work best when you invite people in during a peak in the story. Once they're engaged, you can build the rest of the story in a way that gives your opening sentence context and meaning.

The Pitch-Style Opening Sentence

Have you ever strolled through a carnival before? Pitchmen and women call out to you from all sides, trying to engage your attention in their games or rides.

They use a proven formula for their pitches, and you can use the same for your first sentence. It makes a surprising claim and promises a big result. It looks like this:

[Astonishing Claim] + [Desirable Result]

Examples:

Daily sun exposure could help you avoid doctor visits in the months ahead.

In a case of vacationing your way to success, studies have shown that scheduling more time off is a proven method to achieve your goals.

10 minutes a day is all you need to guarantee income in your retirement.

Because pitch-style opening sentences promise a big result, they keep your reader engaged. Readers wonder how you'll back up your bold claims, and they keep reading so they can find out!

The Suspense-Creating Opening Sentence

The aim of this style of opening sentence is to create impossible-to-resist curiosity about the content to follow. It draws from some of the same aspects of the opening sentence styles we just covered: the storyteller and the pitch. But you may find it simpler to write, and it doesn't involve any special formula.

The effect you want to elicit after the reader reads this style of sentence is for them to wonder, "Wait ... *what?*" You want them to feel they must continue reading so they can resolve the question that's formed in their minds.

You'll accomplish this by saying something that's surprising, mysterious, universally interesting, or a little shocking. That something can be a recently-discovered statistic that will support the point you want to make. It could be the hard-to-believe result your latest client achieved. Or it could simply be a strange analogy that came to mind when thinking about your topic.

Examples:

78% of all Americans believe that standing while working will prolong their lives, and they couldn't be more wrong.

I picked up the phone and heard my long-time client Sam say, "How do I slow down the orders coming in? I can't keep up!"

If you want to get more done every day, approach your to-do list like like you're going to make a sandwich with your time.

The key here is to say something that will create curiosity and make the reader feel compelled to continue to read so they can get their questions answered.

The Compelling Question Opening Sentence

The compelling question opening sentence creates curiosity, too. It asks a question that's provocative and makes your reader think.

Warning: it's easy to get this style wrong. You want to avoid asking a question that can be answered by "yes" or "no." Don't ask, "Have you ever wondered why tea is the most popular drink in the world?" Your reader may respond, "Nope!" and immediately click away.

Instead, building on the concepts we've already talked about, ask questions that seem like the beginning of a story or that create a "Wait … *what?*" reaction. Make a promise that will keep your reader on your page.

Examples:

Did you know there are three foods most of us have eaten all our lives that are proven to increase inflammation and chronic disease?

Have you ever watched some stock prices go through the roof and wish you'd invested in those companies when they were cheaper to buy?

Did you ever wonder why people wait for hours to get inside some restaurants while other places sit empty?

Opening sentences that use compelling questions work when they combine the approaches we've already discussed. They give your reader a sense that they're entering a story that's already underway. They create curiosity that motivates the reader to stay engaged. And they make them want to keep reading to resolve the question you've asked.

The Surprising Statement Opening Sentence

Here's another tried-and-true technique for roping in a reader from the very beginning: make a bold statement that your content promises to back up.

You could base the statement on data you want to share, personal experience, or an anecdote you want to use as an example. The idea is to say something that is a little shocking and unexpected to — you guessed it — create curiosity that will keep them reading your content!

Examples:

65% of our human interactions now happen virtually rather than in person, and the result is we're losing interpersonal skills at an alarming rate.

If I was completely honest with myself, I knew that I had adopted a style of dress that had the result of making me disappear in the eyes of the people around me.

Sarah stepped gingerly onto the stage — expecting her nerves to overwhelm her — and instead was pleasantly surprised to feel right at home.

First Sentence: A Checklist

Help your reader make the transition from your headline into your content with a first sentence that keeps them on the page, engaged in your content.

Master the opening sentence style that feels most comfortable to you, then explore another style. You don't want to bore your readers by starting all your articles the same way.

There are many ways to open an article. The styles covered in this chapter were:

☐ **The Storyteller's Opening Sentence,** which takes the reader directly into a story that's in progress, right at a point of high drama.

☐ **The Pitch-Style Opening Sentence,** which makes an astonishing claim and promises a desirable result.

☐ **The Suspense-Creating Opening Sentence,** which makes a statement that builds curiosity that can only be tamed by reading the article.

☐ **The Compelling Question Opening Sentence,** which asks a question (not a yes-no question) that leaves the reader wondering what you mean — and wanting to read on to clear up their confusion.

☐ **The Surprising Statement Opening Sentence,** which makes a bold claim that will be backed up by the content that follows.

Think about your first sentence as an entity in and of itself. It has an important job to do — it needs to pull your reader from clicking on your headline into engaging in your content. Spend time crafting an opening sentence that will do this important job well.

CHAPTER 8

3. Introduction: How to Get a Commitment to Read

For, usually and fitly, the presence of an introduction is held to imply that there is something of consequence and importance to be introduced. – Arthur Machen

You've hooked a reader. Hurray! They've clicked on your irresistible headline, they've read your first sentence, and they're moving down your page. If we were fishing, I'd say you have one on the line! Time to reel them in.

The job of your introduction is to motivate them to continue reading and dig into the heart of your post. And your introduction section will do this job when you include the ingredients we'll cover in this chapter.

Getting to Know You – and Wanting to Know More

Think about a "real-life" introduction and its purpose. Let's say a friend introduces you to an acquaintance of his whom you've never met before.

Once you get beyond the initial exchange of names and perhaps a handshake, your friend's introduction to the person you're meeting helps communicate basic information about the new acquaintance and establishes *why you should want to talk to them.*

Here's what it sounds like: Your friend says, "I'd like you to meet Taylor. Taylor is a long-time yoga practitioner who's traveled around India. I know you plan to go sometime next year, and I want you two to meet so you can learn more about what it's like to travel to India."

A smart introduction includes why you should interact with the person (or the information) in front of you.

In the previous chapter, we talked about the first sentence of your piece of content. The first sentence is a crucial element because its job is to move the person from the headline into the body of your article.

The introduction section is the first longer section you're asking the reader to consume. Let's take a look at the marks of a successful introduction and talk about what to avoid in this section.

How to Structure an Effective Introduction Section

How long should your introduction be? Let's start with the basics. Your introduction needs to engage the reader and move them along to the rest of your content. *Don't go on and on.* I recommend writing an introduction that's no more than 20 percent of the total words in your post. Even shorter is fine. Your reader is there for the information you'll share — not for the *introduction* to the information.

Give away clues, but not the whole story. Your reader needs to feel motivated to continue to read, so don't give away the conclusion of your article within the introduction section. Leave that for the end.

Give your reader an easy "in." When you're writing your introduction, think about how it *looks* on the page. You want your article to appear easy to read, so aim for short paragraphs of two or three sentences at the most. Don't be afraid to use the occasional one-sentence paragraph — it's like an open door that's easy to walk through.

Aim to sound like a friendly mentor, not a postulating pundit. Use simple, easy-to-understand words and stay away from professional jargon and complex vocabulary.

Communicate with confidence. You want to let the reader know they're going to be in good hands if they keep reading. Let them know that you're convinced about the information you're about to share by writing with a positive, assured tone.

Guidelines for Writing Your Introduction Section

Think about your introduction section like a highway on-ramp. In this part of your article, you're going to get people quickly up to speed by moving them into the bulk of your content.

To help them make this transition from not reading your article to becoming completely engrossed in your writing all the way to the end, there are a few tried-and-true approaches you can use. Use the techniques that follow as starting points — after experimenting with them, you'll have an intuitive feel for the kind of introduction that will work best for individual pieces of content.

In all cases, make sure the intro builds on the first sentence and relates to the rest of the piece. In the previous chapter, we talked about how important the first sentence of an article is, and how to get it right. In your introduction, build on the momentum started with your first sentence — expand the idea and add more detail. Use it to set the tone for the rest of your article.

Promise What They'll Learn and Explain Why They Want to Know It

A highway can be a scary place — trucks whiz by and cars weave in and out. To navigate to your destination, you have to devote your full attention to the task at hand.

To move your reader up the on-ramp and onto the highway of your article, you need to give them a compelling reason to be there. Promise them what they'll learn and describe the problem or challenge your information will solve. Here's what this looks like:

- A **headline** that gets a click.
- A **first sentence** that holds attention.

- An **introduction section** that expands on the problem or challenge and promises a solution by the end of the article.

Draw them in with a surprising or shocking statistic. Your reader needs to understand the significance of the issue you're writing about. One way to illustrate why they should pay attention is to find a verifiable data point that shines a light on the issue at hand.

Here's what this looks like (the figures below are completely made up):

88% of the new websites published this year will be gone from the internet within five years. And that's a shame.

A website represents the hopes and dreams of a person or a business. It's the most convenient way to get the word out about your company.

The sad reality is that the majority of the websites that go offline within five years suffer from the same easy-to-solve problem.

They were never updated with fresh content.

In this article, you'll discover a simple four-step system for creating a website that's a vibrant, irresistible source of information that will be thriving five — and even fifteen — years from now.

Put Forth Two Conflicting Ideas

Ah, *conflict.* It's why we stay tuned in to television dramas. It keeps us glued to movies because we must know how the conflict will be resolved. It causes us to turn page after page of the latest fiction book.

Within the structure of your post, conflict can be used to great effect. And because conflict adds drama, the best place to use it is in your introduction section. It will hook your reader and keep them engaged until the end, where they'll find a resolution to the conflict you set up in the introduction.

In works of fiction, conflict happens when two characters have different ideas about life, different goals in mind, different desires. The two characters end up battling in some way, and we watch from the sidelines as they work it out.

In non-fiction writing, which is what we're focusing on here, conflict happens when you present two ideas that seem to be opposite one another — two views from different angles.

Here's what presenting two conflicting ideas looks like:

We've been told for decades to cover up from the sun — we slather on the sunscreen, wear hats and long-sleeved shirts, and carefully stay out of the noonday heat.

But what if that advice is all wrong?

What if our meager sun exposure has created a new issue — insufficient Vitamin D — which has caused more problems than it has prevented?

The idea here is to present conflicting ideas that you'll resolve in the content that follows.

Take Them Into the Middle of a Story Without Giving Away the Resolution

Weaving a story into your introduction section is an effective way to engage readers. Of course, the story needs to relate to the point you're going to make with your content to be effective.

Even more interesting is to drop readers into the mid-point or end-point of your story, then work backward to explain how you arrived at that place. We see this technique in entertainment all the time — a dramatic scene unfolds before us, and the filmmaker then proceeds to use flashbacks to build the story to the point where we came in.

Here's what this technique looks like in your content marketing:

Every morning during the final week of this past May, I bolted out of bed to check my computer.

My email list was growing by hundreds of people every day that week, and there was no better start to the day than to log on and see the names of the people who had signed up overnight.

I had made a simple change on my website, and that change made all the difference.

In this post, I'll spell out exactly what I did and share a step-by-step template you can use to get similar results.

Use Repetition and the Rule of Three

One way to structure your writing so it has a natural rhythm and confidence is to repeat your points in three ways in your copy.

My years in art school taught me that odd numbers are more pleasing to our eyes than even ones. And three of anything is the first odd number to form a group. It's compelling and convincing. It's not too big, not too small.

You've seen the Rule of Three in use in this book — I use it in my writing without thinking now. Combining the Rule of Three with some artful repetition can drive the point home even more effectively.

Here are a few examples of what this might look like in your own writing:

Repetition and the Rule of Three at work in a single sentence:
New website owners are equally worried about their site's appearance, its functionality, and its growth.

Repetition and the Rule of Three at work in a paragraph:
Preparing for your first hike is easy and fun as long as you keep a few basics in mind. Support your physical experience by packing water and a light snack. Support your personal safety by using the right shoes and following marked paths. And support the memories of your hike by taking along an easy-to-use camera, even if it's simply the one on your phone.

The combination of repetition and the Rule of Three create a compelling, confident, and complete experience of the information you'll share. (See what I did there?)

Use the More Tag Masterfully

If you're using WordPress or other content management system, you'll have access to a tag you can insert at the end of your introduction section that will add a "Read More" message to the end of your introduction.

As you come to the end of your introduction section, be aware of this: some people will come to your blog home page and may only see your article's headline, first sentence, and introduction section before they must click again on the "Read More" link to see the rest of your article.

That means that for a percentage of your readers, you will need to get them past the barrier of yet one more click. So write the final sentence of your introduction — the one just before the More tag — very carefully. Make sure you are creating curiosity again here so that they'll want to "read more" and will be willing to click again to do so.

Introduction: A Checklist

Remember, the goal of the introduction is to move your reader to the main part of your content like an on-ramp moves a driver onto a busy highway.

Aim to write an introduction that is no more than 20 percent of the total words in your article — and shorter is better.

Write with a voice that makes you sound like a friendly, approachable, knowledgeable mentor — not a stiff and unwelcoming hotshot know-it-all.

Use the tips here to craft an introduction that will get your readers up to speed and engaged in your article.

☐ **Defend the importance of the information you'll share.** Back it up with compelling facts and stories of real results.

☐ **Surprise your reader with something they don't know (and don't expect).** Make sure it's related to the main point you'll make in your article.

☐ **Present ideas that conflict with one another.** Set up a conflict in your introduction that will make your reader want to stay tuned so they can see how it's resolved.

☐ **Plop them in the middle or at the end of a good story.** Don't reveal how the story resolves, of course, but talk about the ending and use the rest of the content to build out how the story got there.

☐ **Combine repetition and the Rule of Three for a powerful effect.** Using the Rule of Three and repetition together helps your content sound confident and persuasive. Repeat concepts, repeat words, repeat arguments. It works.

☐ **Master the placement of the More tag.** The More tag is one more barrier some of your readers will need to get past so they can access your full content. Make sure the sentence directly before it is compelling enough to make them want to click "Read More."

CHAPTER 9

4. Subheads:
Delight the Skimmers, Guide the Readers

Subheads break your copy into little potato-chip tasty bites. And we all know how hard it is to stop at just one potato chip. – Sonia Simone

A couple of years ago, I noticed a disturbing trend in my own behavior.

I had always been an avid reader. Libraries were like candy stores to me: so many books, so little time. As I walked among the stacks, it felt like I was walking through physical manifestations of endless possibility, just waiting to be read.

Like many of us, around the dawn of this new millennium I found myself doing a lot of my reading online. Blog posts, online magazines, news sites ... I consumed more words on my laptop screen than I did in books by far.

Once I realized this, I made a vow to myself that I'd go back to reading more books. I wanted to consume longer and more detailed information, the way I used to. I began buying books: print books and ebooks alike. And that's when I noticed a worrisome trend.

I couldn't focus on my reading like I used to.

It was bad — really bad! I could hardly get through a page without finding myself thinking about a related piece of information and grabbing my phone to look it up. It was like I'd forgotten how to read longer pieces because my brain had gotten so used to reading in short bursts.

It turns out that science supports this observation.

Reading On-Screen is Different Than Reading a Book

In a 2005 study directed by Ziming Liu of San Jose State University, researchers analyzed how the digital environment influences how people read on screens. They noticed an emerging "screen-based reading behavior," in which people spend more time scanning and skimming text, reading selectively rather than reading in an in-depth and focused manner.

That's what was happening to me.

Online, we can take advantage of a variety of techniques that will move our readers through our content and pull them down the page until they read the last word. The way we write and format our pages can help readers to consume the information we're sharing.

That's where subheads come in. The job of your subheads is to give skimmers and readers alike a set of highly visible "signposts" they can follow to make their way through your content.

How Subheads Help People Consume Your Content

Subheads are one of the most important ways you can make your online content easier to digest. Let's look at why subheads are so important in today's on-screen reading environment.

Subheads "sell" your content to skimmers. The online reading experience is full of micro-decisions we don't have to make when we're reading a book. Should I follow that link or not? Will I keep reading, or click away? Does this page have what I want, or should look elsewhere? Subheads — when they're written as carefully and consciously as headlines — help to "sell" the content you've written. If someone is skimming a page and deciding whether to read it, compelling subheads will tip the scales in your favor.

Subheads tell a second story. Subheads support what's called the "dual readership path." If we think of the traditional top-to-bottom reader as the first readership path, the second readership path is the one taken by the skimmer. This person looks at the headline, then scrolls down to the first subhead. They may continue to jump from subhead to subhead, deciding all along if they will dive into your content and devote time to reading it — or not. When you construct subheads to appeal to this type of reader (which you'll learn to do in this chapter), you'll draw them in and keep them engaged.

Subheads are a chance to "reset" attention. As mentioned, subheads are like mini-headlines. Using a subhead above a section that has three or four paragraphs allows to you "reset" the attention of your reader, drawing them back into your story in case their attention begins to wander. Subheads are an invitation to re-engage and keep reading.

How to Write Subheads That Pull in Readers

To write the kind of subheads that draw in readers and keep them engaged, you'll need to master a few tips and tricks. You'll be pleased to know that many of the same techniques used for writing great headlines apply to subheads, too. If you've already read the headlines chapter, you're well on your way to writing great subheads.

But subheads don't sit above your content the way headlines do. They're not selling the *entire* article — they're selling one section of it. Here's how to write them.

Give the Reader a Reason to Read the Section Below

Subheads sit like invitations into the content below, and great subheads communicate what the reader will get from reading that particular section. Let's look at some before and after subheads to see what this looks like.

In an article about healthy winter vegetables, you might have a section about tubers, like potatoes and yams. You could choose to use a subhead like this:

Underground surprises for your winter table

And while this is cute and clever … it doesn't make me want to read that section. I have no idea what I'll find there. Instead, you could try these options, which are more specific and communicate the benefit I'll receive from reading the section:

The health benefits of winter tubers (and how often you should eat them)

Winter tubers: how to serve up essential vitamins and delicious flavors

How tubers keep you healthy all year long

All of the options above do a good job of "selling" the content that's in the section to follow. Because I want to be healthy and enjoy delicious foods, these subheads make that section seem like essential reading that I shouldn't skip over.

Move the Skimmer Through Your Narrative

Rather than fight the idea that people skim when reading on a screen, embrace it. Make it easier for skimmers to understand the gist of your content so they can make a decision about whether to spend time reading it from top to bottom.

In addition to enticing readers to consume a particular section of your content, you want to be sure that the subheads, when read independently, tell a compelling story about your article. This is called the "dual readership path," and it acknowledges that some people read subheads independently of the main content.

Write them, drop them in place, and then look at them like a skimmer will — separately. Do they give you a feel for what the content is about? If not, re-write them until they do two things: entice the reader into the section they head up, and engage the reader in the overall article.

Why Write Your Subheads Before Your Main Content?

Well-written subheads form an outline for your content. As I've stated, it doesn't matter what order your content gets written in if you approach your sections as components of a whole. But it *does* help your process if you write subheads before your main content.

Thinking through the order and content of your subheads forces you to create a general outline for your article — a backbone for your information. Doing this before you tackle your main content will make it much easier to write. Later in this book I'll outline a process you can use to get this done — for now, just know that it's subheads before main copy.

How to Format Subheads

One of the first questions I hear about subheads has to do with how to capitalize them. When writing *headlines,* we typically capitalize the most important words they contain, like this:

How to Embrace Your Quirkiness and Build a Profitable Business

Subheads within online content usually use "sentence case" capitalization, where only the first letter in the subhead is capitalized. Subheads don't typically have punctuation at the end unless they are questions.

Here's a subhead from the same article the previous headline came from — note how it's capitalized like a sentence but has no punctuation at the end:

Be loud and proud, and don't be afraid to share who you are

In this article, one of the subheads was a question, so it needed punctuation at the end. It looks like this:

Wait … you too?

And one subhead used two extremely short complete sentences — not something I normally do, but I had to add punctuation when I did. It looks like this:

Seriously weird. And weirdly serious.

And finally, this same article was based on a list of items I shared. To make the list element of the article super obvious, I added numbers to the subheads that were above each point I made. That looked like this:

1. Say your words out loud, and then write them down
2. Shake free from all those rules and regulations

3. Stand on the foundation of your expertise and experience

4. Step out from the shadow of the writers you admire and write it your way

In your site's design, subheads should stand out from the rest of your body text. They should be larger, bolder, and have more space above and below them than a normal line of text. Otherwise, they look like a sentence that's missing punctuation and floating on a page — not good.

Make sure you format your subhead text using the code or setting for subhead text within your content management system. Doing so tells people and search engines that your subhead text is important.

You may notice that this book doesn't follow these subhead capitalization rules! Subheads in books follow different rules than subheads online.

Subheads: A Checklist

Well-written, engaging subheads rely on some of the same techniques used to write compelling headlines. Take another look at the extensive headlines chapter in this book and try some of them when you write your subheads.

Subheads have an additional job to do within your content. Here's how to make them work for you:

☐ **Make a promise that makes the reader want to know more.** Subheads need to promise clear benefits for the section they head up. Don't be clever: you'll just confuse your readers. Let your reader know why they should be interested in the section they're about to read.

☐ **Write for the dual readership path.** Some people will only skim your article and may decide to share it with their audience based on this cursory glance alone. Make sure your subheads tell an independent (and interesting) story in case they're all someone ever reads.

☐ **Format so they stand out.** Subheads shouldn't look like body copy, and they shouldn't look like headlines, either. They should be bolder and larger than body copy. Capitalize the first letter only and don't capitalize any other words.

CHAPTER 10

5. Main Copy: Deliver the Goods

"Make it simple. Make it memorable. Make it inviting to look at. Make it fun to read." – Leo Burnett

It's time for the main event — we're going to dive into the heart of your article. And just like adjusting to cold water in a pool, it's less painful if you jump in fast and start moving right away. You'll warm up before you know it.

Your goal at this stage is to simply *get the words down,* as quickly as possible.

That means you'll focus on writing your first draft fast. You won't worry about editing. You won't go back to polish what you've written at all.

This shouldn't be too difficult. You've already thought through your topic. You have a fantastic headline, and you've mapped out your subheads. You've written your first sentence and the introductory section which is going to make a big promise about how the reader will benefit from consuming your content.

(Remember, you don't absolutely *have* to write in order. If you're just starting out creating content, though, writing your content in this order should make it easier to produce.)

Now, you'll fill in below each subhead. *As fast as you can.*

How to Write Your Main Copy for Effortless Reading

In this chapter, I'm going to show you how to think about your main copy in two different ways.

You'll discover how to write in a way that makes for a smooth reading experience — how to move readers naturally and easily from one section of your content to the next. You'll learn how to weave in stories. I'll show you how to build your information so it supports the idea you're trying to communicate. And I'll share a range for the ideal length for writing online content.

You'll also discover how to make your writing look good. I'm going to introduce this concept here, asking you to keep formatting techniques in mind as you write. And in an upcoming chapter, I'll go into formatting in detail.

The result of this effort will be an article that looks visually inviting.

Even though your reader has clicked on your headline and made it through the introduction, they're still considering clicking away. If your article looks too dense, complex, and daunting, you may lose them.

The Need for Speed

I realize that "write the main copy" sounds like a tall order, but remember — if you've outlined your content with subheads, much of your work is already done.

Writing this main copy is about filling in below those fascinating subheads you wrote in the last chapter. *That's it.*

Still, this is the longest chunk of content you'll write. That's why I recommend aiming for speed at this stage.

The trick to writing your first draft is to pretend you just dove into a cold swimming pool, and your only goal is to get across to the other side where you can dry off with the warm towel that's waiting for you and take a few minutes to sit in the sun.

In other words, you want to get in there and out of there as quickly as possible!

At this stage, your goal is to get the words out of your head and onto your page. You're aiming for what Ann Handley of *Everybody Writes* calls an "ugly first draft." Remember — no one will see this version of your article but you: it's simply a starting point.

Let's talk about how you'll write your main copy.

Weaving in Stories That Support Your Premise

It's no secret that humans are hard-wired to enjoy and respond to stories. From a young age, we tune in to stories that give us insight into life and help us to better understand our world.

Weaving stories into your content is smart — but only when stories support the premise of your article.

You are trying to make a point with your content — to educate, inform, or entertain. If you find a story that will support the goal of your article, by all means, use it.

But if you don't, don't feel you *must* wedge a story into every article you write. You have my permission to write content without telling a story every time.

When you do want to tap into the power of story, however, you'll find the information below helpful.

Great Stories Engage and Open Our Minds

One of the reasons commercials and advertising use stories so often is that when a story begins, people tend to let their guard down and tune in.

Even when our logical minds know without a doubt that we are watching an advertisement, if the ad tells a story, we listen in to see how it develops and how it ends.

Writer and marketer Karen Chronister taught me that great stories consist of three essential parts:

- Two interesting people
- One interesting place
- One conflict (or epiphany, or moment of revelation)

To make your characters interesting, be sure to flesh them out with detailed descriptions. Make them seem real by describing their physical appearance, their motivations, their emotions.

Do the same thing with your interesting location. Invoke as many of the five senses as you can to describe it:

What does it *look* like?
What does it *smell* like?
What does it *sound* like?
What does it *feel* like?
And (if appropriate) what does it *taste* like?

The conflict, epiphany, or moment of revelation adds drama to your story. It's the peak moment. And whether the conflict is resolved or a lesson is learned, it's only once we pass this stage that we feel a sense of completion. The story has been told, and we're better for it.

A few tips for using stories in your content marketing:

Find stories in your own life and the lives of your customers. You know your own stories, so don't be afraid to use them where they support your point. Be sure to tap into the rich resource you have in your own prospect and customer stories, too. Customer stories can become powerful testimonials that help others to visualize themselves interacting with your business.

Use a story in your introduction. Introduce characters and a storyline at the start. Set up a story here, and offer another bit of the story under each of the subheads of your article. Don't resolve it until the summary section at the end.

Start your story in the middle. Consider putting the reader directly into the action by beginning your story in the middle — or just as the action is about to peak — and then filling in the beginning details later on in your article.

Build Your Case, Section by Section

With each section of your article, you want to build the case for the main idea you're trying to communicate.

The most obvious manifestation of this is the list post: your headline features a number, and each subsection of your article has a numbered subhead that shares another chunk of information about your topic or another supporting argument for your premise.

Whether or not you number your subsections, they are — by sharing supporting information and arguments — helping to move the reader to the conclusion you want.

Dole out information subsection by subsection, like stepping stones across a stream.

The information in your subsections will help readers go from where they are now to where you want them to be.

How Long Should Your Article Be?

Most effective content follows a set pattern that looks something like this:

Headline
First sentence
Introductory section: three to five short paragraphs with a "more" tag at the end

Followed by three to five subhead + copy sections that look like this:

Subhead 1
Three to five short paragraphs beneath subhead
Subhead 2
Three to five short paragraphs beneath subhead
Subhead 3
Three to five short paragraphs beneath subhead
Subhead 4
Three to five short paragraphs beneath subhead
Subhead 5
Three to five short paragraphs beneath subhead

Wrapped up with summary and call to action sections:

Summary subhead
One to three short summary paragraphs
Call to action subhead
One paragraph call to action

This is the basic formula we use for Copyblogger posts. It gives you plenty of room to inform, educate, and entertain. We aim for around 1,500 words total, give or take a few hundred words in either direction.

Your mileage may vary, of course. Shorter content (at least 500 words to keep search engines happy) might be best for your audience.

And occasionally, you may want to write an "epic" post that is well over 2,000 words. This might be worth doing when you want to write a post that will serve as a resource you'll link to frequently whenever you talk about a specific topic.

> *For the most part, articles that are about 1,500 words long will serve you very well. They're long enough to make your point and take your readers on a short journey on their way to your main idea.*

At the same time, a 1,500 word article is short enough to be read in just a few minutes, which will make it more likely your readers will read all the way to the end.

Speaking of getting readers to the end, that's what the section that follows will show you how to do.

Moving Your Readers Through Your Content

Believe it or not, even in this middle section of your content the fight for attention and engagement hasn't ended. Your reader can easily click away to something else.

To keep them reading all the way through to the end of your content, use *transition sentences.*

Transition sentences appear at the end of one section, and they foreshadow what the reader will learn in the next section. I just used one at the end of the last section. Did you notice it?

"Speaking of getting readers to the end, that's what the section that follows will show you how to do."

> *Transition sentences make your reader want to stretch their legs out from the stepping stone they're comfortably standing on (the subsection they're in) toward the next stone that will take them across the stream.*

They move readers from the current argument to wanting to know more about the next one. Examples of transition sentences are:

Now that you know how ___ works, let's see what happens when you add ___ to the equation.

Of course ___ is great, but the magic happens when you try ___. Here's what that looks like.

But we weren't done yet. The next thing that happened was ___, and it changed everything.

Not every single section needs a transition sentence. Overuse them and you might begin to sound like a late-night TV pitchman. ("But wait! There's more!")

Sprinkle transition sentences anywhere you feel your reader needs a little extra motivation to keep going. It's an effective way to pull them through your content.

How to Write a Visually Inviting Article

Your content is *seen* before it's read. And your potential readers will make a split-second decision about whether they'll invest time reading it partially based on how it looks.

We are all pressed for time, juggling multiple responsibilities and interruptions throughout our work day. When looking at content, we do a quick mental "ROI" calculation — will I get a return on investment from reading this article? Will it be worth my precious time?

> *One way to win this argument is to create content that has the appearance of a quick read. It looks visually inviting — easy to skim and understand.*

As you write your main content, keep these tips for creating visually inviting content in mind:

Use short sentences. How can you make your sentences shorter? Here's a red flag: if your sentence has an "and" in the middle of it, you can probably chop it into two separate sentences.

Another bad habit I see pretty frequently in online content is indecisiveness about word choice. The writer says something like this:

In recent years, airline travel has become about as unglamorous as riding a bus or taking the metro in a major metropolitan city.

In this case, the writer can't decide which analogy works best, so she uses them both! The sentence would work better if she would make a choice and chop it down to say:

In recent years, airline travel has become about as unglamorous as riding a bus.

If you come up with several ways to say something, *be decisive,* choose the one that's strongest, and let the other go. Your writing will be snappier and more readable when you use your best word choice and eliminate the one that doesn't work as well.

Use short paragraphs. Forget what you learned in English class, and make friends with your "return" key. Break up long paragraphs into short "thought chunks." Any time the direction of thought slightly changes, start a new paragraph.

And don't be afraid to use one-sentence paragraphs occasionally.

Use bulleted lists. Any time you find yourself writing a paragraph with multiple commas or semicolons, look at it again to see if the information could become a bulleted list.

Bulleted lists work best when each bulleted item begins with the same part of speech. They may seem somewhat repetitive, but writing them like this gives them a rhythm that makes them easy to read.

It's easier to understand this if I show you an example. I'm on a plane as I write this chapter, so that's how I came up with my bullets!

An example of sloppy bullets:

- It's hard to be comfortable in a cramped airline seat
- So often, plane trips include delays and missed connections, and this makes it difficult for passengers to rely on air travel
- Your frustration increases the longer your flight lasts

Here's how you can clean up those same bullets simply by shortening the copy and starting each with the object of the sentence:

- Cramped airline seats are uncomfortable
- Delays and missed connections make air travel seem unreliable
- Longer flights mean increased frustration levels

Aim to start all your bullets with the same parts of speech: nouns, verbs, or even adjectives and adverbs. This will set up a rhythm that will make them easier and faster to read.

Use Block Quotes or Call-Outs

Another way to break up your copy visually is to weave in the occasional block quote.

A block quote — like this one — is part of your main copy that you want to give added emphasis to. It should be one to three sentences and formatted to stand out from the rest of your main copy text.

Block quotes are popular with people who are skimming through your article. Along with the headline and subheads, block quotes tend to make people stop and read. I aim for one block quote in each subsection of my main copy area.

Main Copy: A Checklist

Your main copy is what will go below your subheads. It doesn't include your summary or call to action.

☐ **Aim for speed.** Getting your main copy written is a matter of speed: aim for an "ugly" first draft and get it down and done as quickly as possible.

☐ **Tell stories.** They're not essential, but where they work to support your premise, include stories. Fill them with rich detail that includes as many of the five senses as you can.

☐ **Build your case.** Think of your subsections as arguments that you'll use to build your case, slowly but surely.

☐ **Try to keep articles under 1,500 words.** Give or take a few hundred words in either direction, this length gives you enough room to tell your story, make your point, and wrap it up within just a few minutes of your readers' time.

☐ **Use transition sentences.** Pull readers through your content by occasionally using transitional sentences that foreshadow what they're about to read.

☐ **Use short sentences and paragraphs.** Keep sentences short — avoid using "and" in the middle of a sentence. Keep paragraphs short: two-three sentences total, and sprinkle in the occasional one-sentence paragraph.

☐ **Insert bulleted lists.** When a sentence includes comma after comma, replace it with a bulleted list. Start each bullet with a consistent part of speech so they're easy to skim.

☐ **Insert block quotes or call-outs.** Highlight important concepts in your article by styling them as block quotes — text that's styled to stand out from other body copy.

CHAPTER 11

6. Summary:
Wrap Up and Remind

"A word after a word after a word is power." – Margaret Atwood

You know that feeling you get when someone tells you a story that seems like it has no end? It goes on and on. You're not sure what the point is.

But suddenly, they say something that refers to one of the details they shared at the beginning. Your ears perk up. They masterfully wrap up their long-winded story by referring to a point they made earlier, and showing you how they moved you to a new conclusion. They describe the journey from Point A to Point B. You realize the story had a purpose, and you're glad you heard it.

That's the job of a summary.

The summary is a part of successful content you may not have noticed before. It doesn't necessarily say "Summary" above it — it may not even stand apart with its own subhead.

The summary is simply a transition between the most important information you've communicated (your main copy), and the call to action at the end.

If the summary wasn't there, the change from giving information to asking for action would be too abrupt.

A well-written summary gives the reader a sense of satisfaction — they feel they've come full circle with your content. It's not a place to introduce new ideas — it's a place to revisit ideas already introduced.

This chapter is short because your summary can be short, too. I'll share a few tips for writing a good summary and give you some examples and formulas you can try.

By the end, you'll know how to write a summary that creates a smooth shift from sharing information to asking your reader to do something with what they've just learned.

How the Summary Fulfills Your Content's Purpose

The whole point of content marketing is to *move* your reader in some way. The best content causes your reader to:

- Connect emotionally with your business
- Trust your website as a reliable source of information
- Form a new conclusion or think differently about a topic (change their minds)
- Want to take action on something you'll offer in the call to action

Your summary section prepares them for these results by priming their thinking. You'll use it to reinforce the point you want to make and to move the reader gently toward taking an action.

Remember Your Beginning at the End

As you work your way through writing your main content, you may lose track of the stories you told or the facts you shared early on in your article. Your reader may, too.

The best way to bring both of you back to the points you made toward the beginning of your content is to repeat an element of it in your summary section.

- **Did you tell a story in your introduction?** Refer to an element of your story in your summary.
- **Did your article contain five main points?** Refer to those points in your summary.
- **Did your headline contain a memorable word or phrase?** Refer to those words in your summary.

This feeling of coming full circle is very satisfying for a reader. It gives them a sense of accomplishment. They made it through your article, and they have something to show for it! What better feeling to give them just before you're about to ask them to take action?

Remind Your Reader What They Learned

Content marketing shares knowledge in a way that's helpful, interesting, and (sometimes) entertaining. Use your summary to remind your reader about what they just learned. You don't need to rehash the whole article, of course. But hit the main points — *summarize* them! Here are some examples:

Now that you know [information], you will be able to [get desirable result] consistently.

Remember [person, place, or thing mentioned at the beginning of the article]? Here's what happened when they [applied the information just shared].

Next time you decide to [memorable phrase from headline], remember what we talked about here. [Summarize main information shared.]

Remember, your summary should be concise: like a cheat sheet they could use to apply the information you've just shared.

Reinforce How They'll Benefit from Their Newfound Knowledge

The final step in your article will be to ask your reader to take action, and we'll talk about how to do this in detail in the next chapter. To move your reader smoothly toward your call to action, use your summary to reinforce the value of the information they've just received.

Doing so can lead to a feeling of reciprocity. You've given your reader something useful and helpful. They may feel more open to giving *you* something in return, whether that's sharing your content, leaving a comment, registering for your free offer, or even making a purchase.

You can do this in a very natural way by stating it as a wish you have for them, or painting a picture of their future now that they have the information you share. Examples:

My hope is that now that you understand [main point of your article], you'll apply this knowledge so you can [see this desirable result].

So you see, [desirable result] is easier than you may have thought. By carefully following the tips here, like [summarize tips, maybe in a bulleted list], you'll be well on your way.

That [desirable result] isn't so out of reach after all. You can make it happen when you apply [summarize main points].

As you can see, the summary can be just a sentence or two. If you have a lot of points to summarize, consider making them into bullets: readers love to see your main points formatted as an easy-to-skim list.

Begin Establishing Reasons for Taking Action

Because your summary serves as a transition between your main copy and your call to action, use it to "prime the pump" and give your readers a reason to take the action you're about to ask them to take. Of course to do this, you need to know what that action will be! Let's look at some examples:

You want them to share your article:
Now that you've discovered [summarize the main points], why keep it to yourself?

You want them to register for your free ebook about the topic covered in your article:
[Topic] is complex. This article is a great start, but I recommend you read more about this so you fully understand the implications [topic] will have on your business.

You want to ask them to make a small purchase:

Now you know the basics about how [main points] will help you get [desirable result] and why it's important. [Your call to action will tell them how to go beyond the basics.]

These simple transitions set your reader up to move smoothly into the call to action — a challenging content section which we'll cover in detail in the next chapter.

Summary: A Checklist

Your summary moves your reader from learning about a topic to wanting to take action. It's a small — often quite short — transition that smoothly takes them from learning to doing. Here's how to write a summary that sounds effortless and natural:

☐ **Remember your beginning at the end.** Refer to a story told, a headline phrase, or the main points made.

☐ **Remind the reader about what they learned.** Create a feeling of reciprocity by re-stating the knowledge you've shared.

☐ **Reinforce how they'll benefit from what they read.** Paint a picture of the future results your reader can expect once they apply what they've learned.

☐ **Establish reasons to take action.** The section that follows — your call to action — is where you're going to ask your reader for something in return for what you've just shared. Move your reader smoothly toward it by including a mention of why the action matters.

CHAPTER 12

7. Call to Action: How to Get Your Reader to Act

"Consumers do not buy products. They buy product benefits." – David Ogilvy

What was the first thing you ever had to sell? For me, it was Girl Scout cookies.

I was ten years old, dressed in my distinctly unfashionable Girl Scout vest, skirt, and knee socks, walking along the side of the road listening to the gravel crunch under my sneakers. The sun beat down on our neighborhood, and I could smell the melting tar on the road.

I was in a state of abject terror, my sweaty hands clutching a wrinkled order form.

I didn't even know the people whose porches I stood on and whose doorbells I was about to ring: how could I possibly ask them to buy something?

It was horrifying.

I was just a kid who lived on their street. What right did I have to show up and offer something for sale?

It turns out that this lesson from my past taught me almost everything I needed to know to use the right mindset when asking for someone to take action.

At the time, I didn't realize that people *love* Girl Scout cookies. They *want* to buy them. They actually *look forward to ordering them.*

Back then, I didn't know any of that. If I had, I might have ended up being one of the top sellers in my troop. Instead, I was lucky if I could fill in the first ten lines of my order form each year.

Why Calls to Action Matter

Our content — ultimately — has a business purpose. Oh sure, we're writing to attract an audience and build trust. We want to inform and — if possible — entertain. But for our efforts to have a measurable effect on our businesses, we have to take that final step. We have to ask our readers to take action based on what they've read. And we have to sell them on the idea.

That's the job of your call to action. Your call to action is the part of your content where you're going to ask the reader to do something. The action might be to sign up for your free course; buy a product; call for an appointment; register to vote; take a short quiz; download a white paper; or make a small purchase.

In this section, we're going to talk about two components of your call to action: the verbal and the visual. But first, let's talk psychology.

The Psychology of the Call to Action

What's going through your head as you think about writing a call to action for your content? You might be thinking things like, "I don't want to turn people off by asking them to do something." Or, "My readers might unsubscribe from my email list if I start selling them things." Or, "What if I come across as pushy and annoying?"

All common fears. Those are the kinds of thoughts I had when I was trying to sell Girl Scout cookies!

Your readers, on the other hand, are enjoying your content, and they're thinking things like, "This is really helpful. Where can I sign up to get updates from this website?" Or, "I trust this person — they know what they're talking about. I wonder if I can hire them to help me?" Or, "I want to apply what I'm learning on this site to my own business. Is there a product I can buy that will help me do that?"

There are two things happening here — and they're in direct competition with one another. On one side there's you, feeling embarrassed about making an offer. On the other side, there's your audience — wanting to do business with you!

How do we bridge that gap?

It starts with confidence — your confidence.

If you want to create an effective call to action, it should come from a place of knowing your offer is valuable, useful, and helpful to the customer. If you can't honestly say that, work on improving your offer first.

I want you to stand tall and have pride that you have something amazing to offer people. Something they'll enjoy and benefit from.

You owe it to your readers to craft a call to action that will make them want to try your product or service.

To do this successfully, you'll need to pay attention to two aspects: the verbal and the visual. Let's start with the words first.

Your Verbal Call to Action

Calls to action consist of two parts: the words used to make the offer (the verbal part) and the graphic treatment of the call to action (the visual part).

The best calls to action are strong on both levels. They use the right words and combine them with a graphic treatment that makes the call to action stand out visually, so your reader stops and pays attention to it.

When we talk about a call to action, we're not referring to *all the content on a sales page.* Calls to action are a specific section of a larger piece of content. That content could be a sales page, but it could also be a blog post, About page, or your bio.

The call to action is the place where you ask people to act on the information that comes before it. They're usually about 100 words or less. And because the verbal part of your call to action is short, every word needs to count.

There are three parts to a standard call to action: the headline, the offer copy, and the button or link.

The headline: emphasize benefits, not features. The headline should reflect the specific benefits the reader will experience when they take action. This is an important marketing concept that trips up even the most experienced marketers. Your first impulse will be to talk about features, but effective calls to action talk about benefits.

What's the difference? Take a look at this call to action headline which focuses on features:

Get Everyday Citrus Recipes, a 164-page ebook with 100 recipes for using oranges, grape-fruits, tangerines, and clementines at every meal. Click here to buy.

Now take a look at a call to action for the same product which is written to focus on specific benefits:

Bolster your immune system, protect your heart and eyes, and enjoy clearer skin while enjoying the taste of delicious citrus at every meal! Click to get healthy and delicious Everyday Citrus Recipes.

It's tough to pinpoint the benefits, I know. One trick I've used is to ask "why?" In the example above, you could ask "Why incorporate citrus at every meal?" The answer is, *"Because it's good for you."*

Follow that question up. Ask, "Why is it good for you?" The answer is, *"It's good for your immune system, heart, eyes, and skin."*

These are *specific* benefits you can highlight in your headline and body copy. They'll resonate with readers because they touch on what I like to call the "magic five" benefits: Health, Wealth, Relationships, Success, and Peace of Mind.

In the end, what you're offering readers is a better version of themselves in one of these five categories. That means:

- Improved health
- More wealth
- Closer relationships
- Greater success
- More peace of mind and serenity

Tell the reader how your offer's features will *benefit them specifically* in one of these five ways and you can't miss.

The offer copy: be clear, not clever. As you write the copy that will go below your call to action headline, remember — you only have 100 or so words and each one must count. This isn't the time to make a joke or use a clever play on words. Your reader is making an important decision, and you should be ultra clear about why they should take action. If they're at all confused, they won't take action.

Once you've established the specific benefits of taking action, you can weave in features to your call to action. Your benefits will resonate with your readers on an *emotional* level. Weaving in features will help bring *logic* into the picture.

Let's use the same example. In the first sentence, we're highlighting the benefits. In the second sentence, we're backing it up with a mention of the features. It's a powerful emotion + logic combination.

Bolster your immune system, protect your heart and eyes, and enjoy clearer skin while enjoying the taste of delicious citrus! Click to buy Everyday Citrus Recipes — *over 100 recipes for using oranges, grapefruits, tangerines, and clementines at every meal.*

The button: "I want to ___." At the end of your call to action, you'll find a button or a link. This is the physical location on your page or in your email where you're asking the reader to rise to the occasion and take action. It's the moment of truth!

Your button copy makes a difference. Please, please don't wimp out and use the word "Submit" or "Buy" here. Your button or link copy is an opportunity to reinforce the benefits of your offer. Don't miss out.

To write this copy, I like to use the tip I learned from Joanna Wiebe from Copyhackers.com. Joanna recommends you put yourself in your readers' shoes and think about the phrase "I want to ____" when writing your button copy. Fill in the blank with whatever words your reader might use to describe the benefit they'll experience from taking action. To use our example above, we might write, "I want to ..."

Button copy: "Get Healthy and Delicious Citrus Recipes"

You might wonder if writing a call to action is overkill for a blog post. For some pieces of content, a subtle call to action like "Share your favorite ways to use citrus in the comments section" will suffice.

But a great piece of content deserves a stronger, more confident call to action. Why not ask people to sign up for your email list when you've given them a valuable piece of content? Why not tell them about your ebook or your services? Don't be afraid to ask for an action at the end of every piece of content you create.

You might think about it as a spectrum: on the low-commitment end of the spectrum, you may ask them to add a comment or click to read another piece of content on your site. And on the high-commitment end of the spectrum, you may ask them to buy a product, or call to make an appointment.

And remember, when you've got a great product to sell (like Girl Scout cookies) don't be shy about making your offer.

No matter where your call to action falls on the spectrum, people won't act on it if they don't see it. That's what we'll talk about next — how to make your call to action stand out visually.

Your Visual Call to Action

If a call to action is beautifully written but no one sees it, did it ever really happen?

Calls to action, as we've talked about, are short — maybe 100 words at the most. And they usually "live" on a page with hundreds — sometimes thousands — of other words. Your little call to action is outnumbered — it's surrounded by your content. How can you ensure it gets seen?

The key to creating a call to action that doesn't get overlooked is to make it visually different than all the other words on your page. It needs a unique graphic treatment that will stop readers in their tracks and tell them, "This is something you should pay attention to." You don't have to be a designer to make your call to action stand out. Here are the areas to work on.

Use a different color palette. Grab a color wheel, and look at the colors on your website. (Get a free color wheel at bigbrandsystem.com/color). For your call-to-action text, background color, or border (more on this below), use colors that are on the opposite side of the color wheel from the colors people usually see on your site. If your site is all reds and oranges, use blues and greens for your call to action. If it's blues and purples, use gold and orange in your call to action. You may not like how it looks at first. It's going to stick out like a sore thumb! But that's exactly the effect you want.

Make it larger and bolder. Look at the size of your body text. For your call-to-action headline, use at least subhead size text. For the body copy where you share details of your offer, consider using larger-than-usual text, or making it bold. Warning: it will *not* be subtle and beautiful like the rest of your page. And that's a plus.

Surround it with space. Be careful not to bury your call to action inside your page copy. Add space above, below, and to the left and right of your call to action so it floats in the middle of open white space. Doing this will put your call to action on a visual pedestal and help it to stand out.

Use a background or a border. Want to really draw attention to your call to action visually? Add a border or background color to this part of your content. This is a subtle but effective visual trick: by surrounding your call to action with a different color, you're saying, "This is something different: pay attention." Use your color wheel to choose colors that are on the opposite side of the color wheel from what people usually see on your site. Your text needs to be readable, so don't run it on an overly bright or too dark background. Instead, use pale versions of colors. Instead of navy blue, use a light blue tint. Instead of orange, use a light peach tint.

Repeat your call to action, especially if your page is long. If your page is quite long (1,500 words or more), don't be afraid to repeat your call to action.

When deciding where to place repeated calls to action, think in terms of screen real estate. When someone arrives on your page, how many "screens" do they have to scroll through to get to the end? (Yes, I know this will vary according to the screen size, but that doesn't matter for this exercise.) Count how many screens' worth of information and make sure your reader sees a call to action on every couple of "screens" they page through.

Remember, people scan text on the web. On a long page, if you don't feature your call to action more than once, many people will miss it. They'll never scan all the way to the bottom to see your visually prominent call to action sitting like a beacon at the bottom of your page. Call them to action — and don't be afraid to call them more than once.

Marks of an Effective Call to Action: The Checklists

Let's review what you can do to write and design calls to action that get people to act! After all, you're putting a tremendous amount of effort into creating informative, helpful, entertaining content — you deserve to see the business benefits of all this work. The call to action is where the business benefits begin to happen.

Verbal Call-to-Action Checklist

Your verbal call to action has three parts: the headline, the offer copy, and the button or link.

☐ **The headline copy.** Emphasize specific benefits, not features. Ask "why?" to identify specific benefits you can highlight in your headline and body copy.

☐ **The offer copy.** Be clear, not clever. Ask directly and don't include anything here that could be confusing.

☐ **The button or link copy.** "I want to ___." Reinforce what the reader will gain when they take you up on your offer.

Visual Call-to-Action Checklist

Your visual call to action should stand out: make it pop with your design decisions.

☐ **Use a different color palette.** Use colors that are across the color wheel from what people usually see on your site.

☐ **Make it larger and bolder.** Use a larger text size so your call to action stands out from the rest of the copy on the page.

☐ **Surround it with space.** Add open space all around your call to action to "point" people's eyes to it.

☐ **Use a background or a border.** By surrounding your call to action with a different color, you're saying, "This is something different: pay attention."

☐ **Repeat your call to action.** If your page is long, insert a call to action every couple of "screens" your reader needs to page through on their way to the bottom.

Think about your call to action like an on-site salesperson who's representing the best of what your business offers. Spend time making this important element stand out both verbally and visually.

It may seem like a lot of work, but your call to action truly is where business happens! Take care to ensure it's as strong and convincing as it can be so it will work for you day and night, drawing prospects and customers to your business.

Taking Your Content to the Next Level

CHAPTER 13

A System for Easily Publishing Consistently Great Content

Congratulations! You made it through the seven main content sections and now have guidance and tips for writing each one successfully. I'm hoping you'll use them as a reference that you'll keep by your side any time you need to create content.

If you get stuck on writing a section, just flip to your bookmarked page and read the advice for effectively writing that part of your article.

But – How Does This Work in Practice?

I'm glad you asked. It's all well and good to talk about how to write content effectively. But at some point, you've got to *actually do it*. Regularly.

As you know, content marketing works best when it's done consistently over time. One single piece of well-written content won't turn your business around. It's the act of creating and publishing useful content over time that creates business results. Prospects and customers begin to trust you when you show up and are helpful week after week. You become like a wise friend who's always there to lend a hand.

Which, of course, can seem like an incredibly daunting task and an overwhelming commitment. But it doesn't have to be.

In this chapter, I'm going to make the case for creating *less* content, but *better* content. And I'll share my system for publishing high-quality content consistently. It's a system I've used for years, and it made content creation faster, easier, and more fun.

Why Creating Your Content Over Several Days is a Genius Move

Some people reading this book will be part of a team that creates content, and that team may include an editor. Lucky you.

Most of us, though, create our content without the benefit of input from an editor or other team members. For most of us, content creation is a solo act.

That's how it is for me with my content on Big Brand System. I write it myself without any feedback from an editor. And early on, I discovered a way to create that content that allowed my "inner editor" to come to the forefront and improve the articles I was writing.

It all starts by spreading the content creation process out over several days. Doing this gives you a chance to:

Think about your content even when you're not actively writing it. You'll find yourself coming up with a new idea or a different angle when you're working on something unrelated, or even when you're doing something during your off time: watching a television show; washing dishes; taking a walk.

See your content with fresh eyes. Creative "blindness" happens when you've been staring at the same project for too long. It doesn't allow you to see what a piece needs, or notice the errors you've made. Spreading out your content creation process allows you to develop "fresh eyes" again — eyes that can see mistakes. After you've stepped away and done something else, you'll return to your article and notice what's missing or what needs to be changed.

Create content in a stress-free manner. Looming deadlines can be incredibly stressful, and that stress doesn't allow us to do our best work. By starting on the content creation process well in advance and doing it one small step at a time, you give yourself a stress-free environment in which to create. This will support your work and help your ideas to flourish.

The process I'll outline here can be adapted to whatever publishing schedule you use. You may find it interesting to know that even though Copyblogger currently publishes a new piece of content five days a week, no single author writes more than once a week. So when I recommend one strong piece of content per week (as I will below), this advice can apply even to sites that publish more frequently than that.

Why You Should Focus on Creating Less Content – But Better Content

It's true — there's a lot of content on the web already. More is added each day. You may wonder how yours will ever get found and consumed. How can you make your content stand out from the rest?

The answer is to focus on creating content that gets noticed because it's written with the highest standards of quality.

There's already plenty of badly-written, clumsy content out there.

But high-quality content that's written thoughtfully and presented in a way that makes it easy to read and consume? It's rare. Quality content stands out.

> *Great content — well-planned, masterfully written, easy-to-read content —*
> *always rises to the top.*

High-quality content *works,* too. It gets read and acted on. It gets passed around and bookmarked. It gets reader comments and people actually remember it — sometimes for years to come.

If you are working alone and you're creating several pieces of content each week, consider putting all that effort into creating one ultra-high-quality piece of content that's published on the same day each week. The rest of the week can be spent promoting that piece of content and driving people to read it. And once your content is published, you can re-start the system and begin creating the high-quality content you'll publish the next week.

Introducing the 4-Day Content Creation System

When I first started my Big Brand System website, I was running my marketing and design business full time, plus I had two children in high school who were still living at home, and I was keeping a household running. I didn't have a lot of time to spare for content creation, and I certainly didn't have a five-hour (or more) block free to use to create content every week.

At the same time, I knew that publishing content on a consistent basis was the most effective way to get both people and search engines to notice my site. It was how I'd build the audience I wanted to develop for my business.

So I made a commitment to publish one new piece of content once a week. I knew this was a sustainable schedule that I could stick to consistently. And I suspected that fresh content once a week would be enough.

It was. Over the years, my audience grew, slowly but surely. When I first drew back the curtains on my website, there weren't many people out there watching. But that changed quickly as I began consistently publishing helpful, useful, easy-to-read content.

> *Because I didn't have big chunks of time available to write content, I developed a system that entailed spreading the content creation process over a period of days rather than creating content from start to finish in one sitting.*

It turns out, this adaptive behavior was a highly efficient way to create quality content week after week.

In this chapter, I'm going to present my system for creating content over a period of four days:

Day 1: Build Your Article Backbone.
Day 2: Fill in the Details.
Day 3: Polish and Prepare to Publish.
Day 4: Publish, Promote, and Propagate.

Out of sheer necessity, I developed my strange system for getting content created.

And, as often happens when inventions are born from necessity, I hit on something that worked even better than sitting down and trying to write an epic piece of content in one single session.

In May 2012, a little over two years after I started my online business, I wrote about my weird little content creation system in what has turned into one of the more popular posts on Copyblogger: A Simple Plan for Writing One Powerful Piece of Online Content per Week.

The positive response that post received is one of the reasons you're reading this book. It gave me the confidence to think that maybe I could actually teach people how to write content — even though I had just learned myself.

I'm going to share it with you here with some additional details that will help you put it into practice. It all starts with deciding which day you want to publish, and working backward from there.

What Day Should You Publish Your Weekly Post?

This system starts with finding a consistent day every week when you'll publish your content. A few considerations for choosing your publishing day:

Think about a convenient day for your reader, not for you. It's tempting to say, "I want to publish on ___day, because that day works best with *my* schedule. But it's not about you, is it? You're publishing content because you want to reach an audience. Think about what will work best for them, and work your schedule around that. Read on for more about this.

If your content is time-sensitive, publish it on the day it will be most useful. Let's say your website features information about the latest happenings for antiques lovers in your region. You talk about sales, events, workshops, and new stores that have opened up in your area. You know that your readers do most of their antiquing on the weekend. When are they making their weekend plans? Probably on Thursday — or Friday morning at the latest.

Publish your content on the day it's most likely to be useful to your readers. Think about how they'll apply the information you're sharing and when during the week they most need it.

Look for a traffic pattern in your site analytics. If your publishing schedule has been willy-nilly or non-existent, take a look at your site analytics. Is there a consistent spike in visits to your site on a specific day of the week? If so, make the most of existing traffic patterns by publishing a new piece of content that day.

In the end, you may find that none of the guidance above helps you choose a publishing day. In that case, it's time to make an educated guess. Think about your audience first, and choose a day you expect will work for them. Plan to review your traffic after a few months to see if it spikes on the day you publish (that's a good sign). You can even do a short audience survey to ask your readers what day they prefer to see new content from you and then look for a pattern in their answers.

With your publishing day chosen, work backward three business days. If you're publishing on Friday, you'll start your four-day process on Tuesday. If you're publishing on Tuesday, you'll start your four-day process on Thursday of the week before (take the weekend off!).

Once you know what day you'll start, read on to see what to focus on during the first day.

Day 1: Build Your Article Backbone

On the first day of your content creation process, you're going to choose your topic and create what I call the "backbone" of your post.

If you've followed the advice in the content strategy chapter, you already have a content idea library. You don't have to spend time staring out the window, waiting for an idea to hit you — you have content ideas to draw from and can easily find something to write about.

With your content topic in hand, let's create the backbone of your article, which consists of two parts: your headline, and your subheads.

Write your headline

As we talked about in the headline chapter, your headline is the most important promotional part of your content. Your headline is what gets people to click on your content and read it.

Spend plenty of time generating lots of headline ideas.

When I write headlines, I like to think of writing the first 10-20 headline ideas like clearing a clog in a pipe: once you get the "junk" ideas out of the way, the good ideas can flow. So don't worry if your first attempts at headlines are dull, or clichéd, or boring. Just get them out of your system so the good stuff can flow through, and *keep writing*.

Writing great headlines becomes easier and more natural the more you do it, so keep at it. For more guidance on writing headlines, refer to the headlines chapter in this book.

Write your subheads

After you've written your headline, map out the subheads you'll use in your article.

Subheads are like signposts that guide your reader through your content.

But they're also signposts for you, the writer! Writing subheads at this early stage of the game helps you to think through how you will present and develop the ideas you want to communicate in the piece.

If you're aiming for around 1,500 words for your article, you could write five or six subheads.

For more on writing subheads, review the Subheads chapter in this book.

Day 1 Tips

Tools to use: I like to keep it simple, and I tend to do everything on my laptop. But because some people strongly prefer to interact with tangible objects like pen and paper, I'll make recommendations for both.

My writing life changed for the better when I incorporated mind mapping tools into my process. Any mind mapping software will do: find one that looks good, seems easy to use, and fits your budget (many are free).

The reason I love mind maps so much is they allow me to get ideas out of my head quickly and easily, and move them into a format where I can work with them. My ideas don't come to me in a linear or logical order (do yours?). I don't fret about that — I just use the mind map to record them in whatever order they appear.

When I'm done thinking, I begin moving things around on the mind map to arrange them into an order that makes sense. As I move things, I notice gaps in my thinking, and I fill those in with more ideas.

In the end — once I have my ideas arranged — I can see what subheads are needed. Some of my main ideas can be lightly edited to turn into subheads.

If you prefer to work with tangible objects, you could use index cards or sticky notes. I have a friend who makes major decisions by standing in front of a window with a pad of square sticky notes, jotting down short concepts with a marker and sticking the notes to the window, moving them around and grouping them together until she can see what she needs to do.

Some people swear by a combination of colored and white index cards arranged on a table top. Remember, you're just jotting down main ideas at this stage, so don't feel like you need to fill the lines on your index cards if you use them. Jot a concept across the top and that's it.

Use whatever system works best for you. Remember, *the magic isn't in the tools you use — it's in what you do with them.* So don't get hung up on trying a bunch of different tools or techniques: find one that works and stick with it.

Once you've finished writing a compelling headline and strong subheads, you are done with Day 1. Walk away and go about the rest of your day. Your mind will continue to work on the content — you may get ideas about it when you're working on completely unrelated tasks. Find a way to save those ideas: you'll need them for tomorrow's work.

Here's the sneaky thing about your Day 1 tasks: by the time you finish, what you've created is an outline of your article. But since most of us are still recovering from having to generate outlines for our term papers in English class, we won't call it an outline. Instead, think about it as the *backbone* of your content. You've created the main structure you'll hang the rest of your content on. It's the foundation of your article. Good job!

Day 2: Fill in the Details

If you're a coffee or tea drinker, Day 2 might be a good day to drink an extra cup. You're going to write a lot today, so do whatever it takes to go into the day with your energy high.

The first thing to do on Day 2 is to review the headline and subheads you wrote the day before. You're seeing them with fresh eyes now — do they still make sense? Do they sound intriguing? Do you feel excited about writing what's missing? (If so, that's a good sign.)

If you see weaknesses in your basic structure, take some time to fix them before you start to write. Reinforce your structure so it's strong enough to support the words you're about to hang on it.

Once you're happy with the headlines and subheads, it's time to fill in the details.

Ready? Set? Write!

Write your first draft

I know this sounds ridiculous, but I want you to think of your Day 2 work like a race. And there's a good reason for this.

On Day 2, your goal is to write the first draft of your article. This is a stage where you might get stuck: after all, writing a first draft feels like *actually writing your content.*

And it is, but I want you to keep it in perspective at this stage. What you're writing is a messy, junky first draft. It doesn't need to be perfect. It won't seem polished.

What it needs to be — by the end of Day 2 — is done.

Done is way more important than *perfect* at this stage. Remember: no one is going to see this except you.

So write, write, write. *Do not go back and edit.* Don't attempt to polish and perfect what you've written. Write forward, not backward.

Day 2 Tips

Write your first sentence. This book contains a whole chapter on writing compelling first sentences. I know — overkill, right? But the first sentence is an important transition element that will pull your reader from your headline into your content, so don't skimp on this handful of words.

Write your introduction section. Your introduction section is equally important. Your reader is making a decision about whether he or she should spend time reading the rest of your article. Your introduction section should sell the benefits they'll gain from reading your content. Review the Introduction chapter for help with this section.

Fill in under your subheads. You've thought through your content structure and written compelling subheads. Now fill in a first-draft version of the text that will go beneath each subhead to explain the point you want to make. See the Main Copy chapter for guidance.

Write your summary. Wrap it all up with a summary that refers to your main points and shows your reader the journey they've taken. The Summary chapter will help you write this part.

Add a call to action. Remember, all content includes a call to action, even if all you do is ask for comments. Think through this important interaction and get more information about how to effectively write it in the Call to Action chapter.

Remember at this stage, *don't sweat the details.* Just get your thoughts down, and don't edit anything. You have a full day reserved for editing, and you'll do a better job editing if you leave some time between the writing stage and the editing stage anyway.

Whew! That was a lot of work in one day. It's time to walk away from your content. Once you've written your first draft, you can feel satisfied that you've gotten your thoughts down. Do something else and get a good night's rest because you'll need fresh, rested eyes to do the next day's work.

Day 3: Polish and Prepare to Publish

Day 3 is the last day before publishing, so everything you do on this day will be to prepare your content to go out into the world and to give it the best possible chance of being consumed.

Review your draft and clean it up

At this point, you've seen your content over a couple of days. Hopefully, this extra time has given your mind a chance to mull over your subject and surface new ways of explaining it. That's the beauty of this system — you give yourself time and space to develop your best work.

Day 3 Tips

Start the day with a quick read-through to see how your content looks today.

My favorite way to do this is to read it out loud in a monotone voice. If your content still makes sense and sounds good — even with no inflection in your voice — you're in good shape. If something sounds confusing or unclear when you read it this way, make edits until it is easy to understand.

At this stage, you want to edit and carefully proofread for typos and grammatical errors. Consider reading your content from top to bottom and then from bottom to top — sometimes reading it in opposite order helps mistakes to come to the forefront. Keep reading and tweaking until it's just right.

Next, spend some time formatting your post for readability. Remember, we read differently online: our eyes scan text. Everything you can do to inject your content with ample subheads, bulleted lists, and block quotes (or call out quotes) will help encourage your readers to consume your information.

Be generous with your return key. Break up long paragraphs into shorter, more compact "thought chunks." Every place you see a thought "turn a corner" and head in a different direction, hit the return key. Don't be afraid to to feature a one-sentence paragraph occasionally: when you want to highlight an idea, this is a great way to draw attention to it.

Add bulleted lists. Look for sentences that contain lots of consecutive commas. For example, when you think about flavors of ice cream, do you think of smooth vanilla, sweet strawberry, creamy chocolate, luscious caramel swirl, and crunchy rocky road? Instead of the previous sentence, do this:

When you think about flavors of ice cream, do you think of:

- Smooth vanilla
- Sweet strawberry
- Creamy chocolate

- Luscious caramel swirl
- Crunchy rocky road

As you can see, the bulleted list injects a lot of white space into your page. It's fast and easy to skim. Read more about writing easy-to-read bulleted lists in the Main Copy chapter of this book.

Add excerpts using block quotes. Block quotes or call-outs highlight specific excerpts of text that you'd like your reader to notice.

> *This is an example of a block quote which is styled differently than the text above and below it. It highlights something special you don't want your reader to miss.*

The beauty of these stylish chunks of text is that they are surrounded by white space, so your reader's eyes go straight to them. Because they're formatted differently from the surrounding text, they stand out.

When you're thinking about which text to highlight in a block quote, use the same thinking we use about subheads. When read separately from your content, subheads tell a story all on their own. Block quotes do this, too.

So as you pull out a sentence or two to highlight in a block quote, think about the overall message your reader will understand if all they ever read are your block quotes. Your block quotes will stand out as people scan your text — will they invite skimmers to read?

Add an image. The next chapter covers images in detail. On this final day of polishing your post, find an image that conveys the meaning of your content in visual form.

Day 4: Publish, Promote, and Propagate

It's your fourth and final content production day: time to hit publish!

Your content marketing job doesn't end on the day your article goes live. In many ways, it's just the beginning of your efforts to make sure your information gets in front of as many people as possible.

Day 4 Tips

Publication day is the day your content promotion process starts. This article you spent three days crafting deserves attention, and it's your job to ensure it gets it.

How can you do that? Try:

- Making yourself available in your comments section to answer questions and interact with your readers. When readers see the author is available, they tend to show up and speak freely.
- Promoting your post across the social media channels you use: don't be afraid to post multiple times on the day of publication.
- Emailing your article to your list of readers or including it in your email newsletter.
- Going back to previously-published content that gets traffic and "linking forward" to this content when it complements the information on the previously-published page.

Not all content fits in the "epic" category. But when you write an especially good article that you know would help a specific group of people, reach out to other website owners and ask them to share your content with their audience.

To do this, consider sending a message that sounds like this (feel free to add details):

Hi [NAME],

I have learned so much from reading your site, [URL]. Thank you.

You share valuable information about [TOPIC], so I thought you might want to share my latest article, [HEADLINE and LINK] with your readers. The focus of this piece is to help readers [HOW THEY'LL BENEFIT FROM READING].

I appreciate anything you can do to help me get this content into the hands of the people who need it: thanks in advance for your help.
Best wishes,
[YOUR NAME]

It's not easy to write strong content week after week, but dividing the work up over several days makes it feel less daunting. And building time into your schedule to step away from your post and return with fresh eyes will make you a better writer and editor.

To make this system work, decide on the day you'll publish and put it into your calendar as a repeating event. Then set up repeating events for your Day 1 tasks (Build Your Article Backbone); your Day 2 tasks (Fill in the Details); your Day 3 tasks (Polish and Prepare to Publish); and your Day 4 tasks (Publish, Promote, and Propagate).

Feel Free to Ignore This System

One important note: if you are not a "systems" person, and you find processes like this too constraining, please don't feel like you "must" follow the information in this chapter to create your content.

This system has worked beautifully for me, and some of my best content has been created when I use it. But I don't write every single piece of content this way — sometimes a deadline looms and there simply isn't time to spread the content creation process out over time like this.

In those cases, I still end up using these basic steps, but the time between them is condensed. For example, I still try to write forward when I write my first draft — not allowing myself to go back and edit as I'm writing. And I still build in time between writing and editing … but sometimes instead of 24 hours, it's a 30-minute lunch break that gives me enough time to think about something else and return to the content with fresh eyes which are ready to edit.

In a perfect world, you would spread out your content creation process over a three-day period. But we don't live in a perfect world, do we? So follow this system when you can, and when you can't, don't worry about it.

Does Your Article Rely on Research? Start with a "Day 0"

Not all content is based on extensive research, but some definitely is. You may write research-based articles all the time, or only occasionally.

Either way, if you need to add research to the mix, plan on adding a "Day 0" to your content creation system. On Day 0, spend time gathering resources and taking notes so you'll have what you need when it's time to write your headlines and subheads on Day 1.

Checklist: A System for Publishing Great Content

Focus on creating less content, but higher-quality content. There's always room for well-written and beautifully presented information — the best content rises to the top.

☐ **Spread your content creation process out over four days.** This gives you space and time to do your best work.

☐ **Day 1: Build your article backbone.** Pick your topic and focus on writing an engaging headline and strong subheads.

☐ **Day 2: Fill in the details.** Fill in the structure you created on Day 1 with all your main copy: focus on speed and aim for first-draft quality (remember, no one will see this stage).

☐ **Day 3: Polish and prepare to publish.** Do a careful read-through to proofread and polish your article. Spend some time formatting it for readability. And choose an image that will communicate and intrigue readers. (More on this in the next chapter.)

☐ **Day 4: Publish, promote, and propagate.** Use this final day to put your article into circulation on social media. Give it a good push on the day of publication, repeating your posts about it several times on the platforms you use. Then add it to your long-term social media promotions, so you continue to drive readers to your content over time.

CHAPTER 14

How to Use Images to Enhance Your Content

*"You must give birth to your images. They are the future waiting to be born ...
fear not the strangeness you feel. The future must enter into you long before
it happens ... Just wait for the birth ... for the hour of new clarity."*
– Rainer Maria Rilke

If you're not a working artist, this chapter may push you straight out of your comfort zone. "Me? Create images for my content? No way."

The good news is that image creation (just like content creation) can be learned. I'll share a few rules of thumb to guide you as you get started. When you combine the rules I'll teach with practice, you'll become more proficient with image creation over time.

You may even find yourself looking forward to creating images! I believe that's partly because images are processed in a different part of your brain than words. When you work on your images, you're giving that hard-working verbal processing center a break.

Your Visual Cortex: An Unsung Superhero

Your visual cortex is a small part of your brain that's hidden toward the back of your head. But its effects are massive: it produces the reality you see all around you. And it's fast: it processes visual information 60,000 times faster than words.

Images "speak" a different language than words and convey their meaning faster, too. That's why one of the most important things you can do to put a finishing touch on any piece of content is to add an image.

One of your goals is to create content that gets noticed and read, and great images make us stop and look. There's proof for this: a 2013 study by MDG Advertising showed that content featuring compelling images averages 94 percent more total views than content without.

But images don't just draw viewers — they boost understanding (and retention), too.

Text and oral presentations are not just slightly less efficient than pictures for retaining certain types of information; they are much less efficient. If information is presented orally, people remember about 10 percent, tested 72 hours after exposure. That figure goes up to 65 percent if you add a picture.
— John Medina, Brain Rules

Images Invite, Explain, and Entertain

The best images add meaning to the words you've written: they convey emotion, evoke an atmosphere, and communicate opinions. All this without words! It sounds like a tall order, but the information in this chapter will help you find and use images that do all that.

You've spent time and effort writing an amazing article. Let's put some icing on that cake with an image that draws attention to the content you created and helps boost comprehension, too.

Revisit Your Carefree Image Creation Days

As young children, we all start out as artists. The difference between the art we made when we were kids and the art we make now is that when we were kids, we didn't care about whether our images "worked." We enjoyed creating them, and that was all that mattered.

There's no time like today to revisit your inner artist. And there are good business reasons to start adding images to your content.

Image processing happens in a different part of the brain from where words are processed, so putting images with your words will engage more of your reader's brain.

Images are especially effective vehicles to activate associations. If you spark an experience or memory with your image, you can convey a meaning that goes well beyond the words on the page.

Block Out Time to Find the Best Image

Recreate those carefree "artist" days by blocking out time for image creation in your schedule. Some people like to "warm up" with images as the first thing they do when they get into their office in the morning. Others identify the times of day their minds seem to need a break from writing words or doing calculations, and they use those times to create images.

I jump between writing and creating images all day long. I look at my to-do list and check in with myself: "Am I in the mood for writing, or creating images?"

Begin with a Goal

What exactly do you want to accomplish with the image in your piece of content? What effect would you like it to have?

When they're created for marketing our businesses, our image goals fall into common categories. We want to:

- **Entertain:** these images provoke smiles and spread goodwill
- **Educate:** these images share information and build authority
- **Provoke:** these images surprise and prompt an action
- **Inspire:** these images evoke emotion, encourage, or uplift the viewer

Decide what you want to communicate from one of the categories above and choose an image as a vehicle for your message. Having this information in hand will make it easier to get through the next step without wasting time.

Where to Avoid Looking for Images for Your Content

Before I talk about where to look for images, I want to talk about where *not* to look for images. And to do that, I need to share a few words about copyright. Stick with me! It will be short.

Literature, art, and photography are intellectual property which benefits from the protection of copyright. Finding an image floating around on the web doesn't grant you the right to use it: someone owns it, and you may only use it if the owner gives you permission.

This permission is often conditional. For example, you may be allowed to use an image to illustrate a point in a purely editorial context, but you may not be able to use it in a commercial context.

I have known several people who have been sued for not paying attention to proper usage. They ended up owing thousands of dollars to the owner of an image because they used it without paying for it, thinking they had permission. These people didn't set out to "steal" anything, but that's exactly what they did.

Never use a web browser's image search function to find images to use in your content. It is too tempting to find the "perfect" rights-protected image there. I also recommend you avoid image-sharing services like Flickr. Yes, some photographers add a Creative Commons license to their images which grants permission to use it. But I knew someone who used an image with a Creative Commons license and then, later on, the photographer changed the license and my friend had to stop using the image. It was an image that had been used to sell one of her well-known products for many years, and she had to scramble to look for a replacement.

Let's keep you out of legal hot water and save you from future headaches, shall we? Here's how to find images you have the right to use freely — images that will make your content more attractive and effective.

Where to Look for Images for Your Content

To find the perfect image for your next piece of content, you have three choices:

- **Find** a free stock photo you have the rights to use.
- **Buy** a high-quality stock photo you have the rights to use.
- **Create** an image yourself.

You can also commission photography, of course, but that's not very common for web content. Even major corporations use high-quality purchased stock photography. Let's look at each of these three choices in detail.

Free Stock Photography

An important note: when looking at free stock photography, be sure to check the licensing on any image you use. In many cases, the image is free to use in exchange for crediting the photographer who provided it. Sites will specify what you need to say in the photo credit, so follow their directions carefully.

Pixabay.com: Pixabay is my favorite free photo site because it's the one that feels most like a paid site. It features easy-to-search photos, illustrations, and vectors. Pixabay images are vetted by a team of volunteer editors and do not require you to credit the photographer. Creating an account on the site will allow you quicker access to images, which you can download in a variety of sizes.

Kaboompics.com: Kaboompics offers major image categories and has a search feature, too. Their image collection isn't huge, but the images they do have are high-quality and quite large — large enough to be used for print design. The only thing you can't do with Kaboompics images is to sell them: the site is devoted to keeping their images free.

TheStocks.im: TheStocks is a collection of stock photo sites all in one place — the majority of which are free. You can use the interface to browse collections and get a feel for the quality and style of the photos available.

Paid Stock Photography

Over the years that I've taught branding, I've met a few people who didn't ever want to pay for the photography they used. And I have to confess I got more than a little impatient with them.

You see, I have art directed more photo shoots than I can remember. And I know how much work happens to create the professional-level images featured on paid stock photography sites.

Memorable images aren't easy to create, and I think the hard work is worth paying for.

When you're ready to make a very small investment in getting professional photography that you have the rights to use for any commercial purpose — and that you can run without adding a photo credit — take a look at these paid stock photo sites:

Bigstock.com: I love the oversized images, advanced search features, and vast archive on this site. It's my go-to when I need an image that stands out.

Shutterstock.com: Polished, beautiful images with a robust search feature.

Adobe Stock: A massive collection of high-quality images with a price range that reflects the quality (it's on the high side). Worth looking through when you need a specific image that will be memorable.

Create Your Own Images

Here's a radical idea. Chances are very good that you walk around every day with a camera close by in the form of your smartphone.

What would happen if you began registering images of the world around you, a few photos at a time?

When you're looking around, keep your eyes open for:

- **Contrast:** Look for color contrast, light and shadow contrast, size or texture contrast.
- **Faces and emotions:** Keep your finger on your camera button to capture expressions, emotions, and stolen glances that tell stories.
- **Angles:** Dramatic angles and a sense of perspective that draw your eye into the image make a boring image interesting. Sometimes all it takes is positioning yourself or your camera above, below, or to the side for the image to come to life.

The Art of Image Searching

Some images just work: they complement your words; they add shades of meaning and entertainment value to your page.

And some images? They're boring, they send the wrong message, and they aren't worth spending time deciphering.

Jakob Nielsen of the Nielsen Norman group, which is devoted to researching website usability, says this about images:

"Users pay attention to information-carrying images that show content that's relevant to the task at hand. And users ignore purely decorative images that don't add real content to the page. So much fluff — of which there's too much already on the web."

To find the best images, you'll want to become skilled at searching for them. Here are the tips the pros use:

Start searching for one word, then narrow your results by adding words or subtracting. Searching a single word usually leads to an overwhelming number of results. Bring up the results from a single-word search, and see what you want more or less of. Most sites will allow you to add a minus sign before terms you don't want to appear. If you're getting a lot of results with children, for example, and you're looking for an image of business people, add "-children" to the search box along with your original word.

Use style terms. Adding specific words like "vintage," "grunge," "white background," or "close up" will narrow down your results. You can also narrow your results by orientation, so you only see vertical or horizontal images.

Step back and see what jumps out. When looking at a page of thumbnail images, ask yourself, "Which one stands out?" When an image holds its own among dozens of others, that's a good sign that you've found a strong one.

Consider your text. If you plan to add text to your image, look carefully to ensure there's an open area on the photo that doesn't have a lot of busy text underneath it, so your text will be readable.

Consider where the image "points." Many images look like they "point" a certain way. Sometimes a person in the image is looking off to the right, left, above, or below. Viewers will tend to follow their gaze. Sometimes the image has strong angles that send viewers' eyes in a specific direction like they're following an arrow. Make sure to use this to your advantage: position images so they draw viewers toward the text you want them to read. For more on this, search for an article called Point Out the Obvious with Images on Big Brand System.

Use a single focal point for high drama. The most dramatic images have a single focal point: an obvious visual "star of the show." Sometimes you can achieve this manually by cropping an image to remove extraneous elements and focus your viewers' eyes.

Using Images: A Checklist

☐ **Search with a goal in mind.** Get clear on what you want to accomplish with the image you'll add to your content before you search.

☐ **Don't get in legal hot water by searching in the wrong place.** Make sure you have full rights to every image you use.

☐ **Explore free stock photos.** Be sure to follow any requirements for photo credits and links.

☐ **Buy stock images.** For a small fee, you can find the perfect image for the job in the vast archives of stock photo sites.

☐ **Create images yourself.** Use your phone's camera to begin recording the world around you and consider using your unique images in your content.

☐ **Search like a pro.** Use the tips in this chapter to make your image searches faster and more targeted, so you'll find the exact image you need in record time.

Want to know more about images? Visit bigbrandsystem.com/design/images/ to read my image-related articles.

CHAPTER 15

Content Strategy for the Long Haul

And the end of all our exploring
Will be to arrive where we started
And know the place for the first time.
— T. S. Eliot

At this point in our time together, I'm hoping you're feeling much more confident about the content creation process. I hope you have a sense of excitement about trying some of the new techniques you've learned and implementing the ideas I've shared.

As we wrap things up, I want to spend some time helping you to look ahead.

Because content marketing works best when you keep at it over time. The content you create is like a brick building — your first content forms the foundation. The longer you add content, the larger and more impressive you make your web presence.

Well, especially if the bricks you build with actually fit with the others and look and feel related! If you add bricks, but also wood, stone, and ceramic tile, people will be thoroughly confused when they find you on the web.

Let's avoid that confusing fate and talk about how to ensure that past content and
future content work together to support where you want to take your business.

This doesn't mean that your interests and focus can't evolve over time — they most certainly will, and this is healthy. What I want to help you avoid is a site that's a mishmash of unrelated content. Even though you'll create it over time, let's make sure your content is cohesive and powerful now and in the future.

Use Your Categories List as a Guide

In the earlier content strategy chapter in this book, we talked about coming up with a categories list for your site. I encouraged you to develop a handful of representative categories at first and to add to that list as needed over time with a long-term goal of no more than eight to ten categories total.

Your categories list is like a restaurant menu — within the menu categories there is plenty of room for creativity and experimentation. But the overall category list serves to orient your reader about what you offer as a whole. And it helps guide you, the content creator, so your content doesn't go off in a direction that doesn't support your business goals.

Think Beginner, Intermediate, Advanced

There's a fascinating phenomenon that happens as you write about a topic over many weeks, months, and years. Over time, you naturally become more knowledgeable about it. Teaching a topic has this effect! You increase your mastery and understanding of a subject when you educate others about it.

The danger in this situation is that you may start out writing content that's perfect for beginner and intermediate readers. As your mastery grows, you begin to cover topics that are for more advanced readers. At this point, you may find it difficult to remember what it was like to be a beginner. You may lose touch with the kinds of questions beginners have.

In the chapter about matching your content to your customer's journey, we talked about beginner, intermediate, and advanced content. How can you keep your readers' awareness level in mind as you plan your content?

Review the basic reader questions that we talked about in that chapter. Here they are to jog your memory:

- Beginner: **What is ___?**
- Intermediate: **How do I do ___?**
- Advanced: **How do I get better at ___?**

Remember, beginners don't even know what your topic entails or why it's important. Create content for them that supplies that meaning and context.

Intermediate and advanced readers want to put your information to use and build mastery.

How Your Content Needs Will Change Over Time

You set out to create content for your website using the categories and topics you develop, but then one day you realize things have changed:

- Your business has begun to offer a new product or service.
- Your ideal customer has changed, and you want to reach a different group of people.
- You need to reposition your business in the market: maybe so you can charge more, or maybe to establish authority around a new topic.

This is a natural result of being in business, and it's perfectly fine! Rather than thinking you need to pull apart everything you've accomplished so far, let's think about ways you can build on your efforts and move toward the new goals you've set for yourself.

How to Pivot Your Content Topic

It's possible that you'll begin writing about the wildlife of the Australian plains and then decide you want to write about baking vegan cupcakes. In that case, the advice here won't work.

It's much more likely that your *focus* will change — that you'll decide to train your attention on a slightly different aspect of the topic you normally write about. I call that a content pivot, and the advice here will help you achieve it with grace.

Be honest: introduce your new area of focus or interest. Explain why you want to explore it. Explain how your readers will benefit. Encourage questions.

Write about your new topics, but relate them to your established topics. Find ways to tie your new focus back to your previous one. This will help readers see your content as a body of work that focuses on different elements of a whole.

Re-visit older topics occasionally. If you can, incorporate your previous topics and feature them occasionally in your newer content. Again — try to weave the old and new together, so readers understand how they're related.

"Power Boost" your Best Content

Certain pieces of content will take off. I wish I could tell you why this happens, or how you can predict it. But there's absolutely no predicting it — sometimes the article you least expect goes viral and is widely shared. The page becomes one of the most visited on your site.

And sometimes the article you spend hours of time and loads of effort on does nothing.

It's a good idea to see if there's a common trait between all your most-visited pages: are they tutorials? Do they share personal stories? Are they software or book reviews? If you can see a pattern between them, you may find a way to build on the success and create more content along those lines.

When you find a content "winner," there are several ways to leverage that success to get the best results possible.

Write guest posts on the topic (and link back to your original content). Approach other site owners and volunteer to write content on their sites that covers the topic. Point back to your popular post when making the pitch, and then link to the post when you write your guest article.

Make the post into a landing page. Landing pages are stripped of navigation menus and other distracting elements so the viewer can focus on the offer made. Take your popular content and, using the same URL, set it up on a landing page with an offer. Share your information and add a call to action to sign up to an email list, purchase a small product, or contact your business.

Feature the content in your "best of" sidebar. Send new site visitors to your top content when you feature it in the sidebar of your site.

Put the page into rotation on social media. Your audience has told you it likes a piece of content, so keep it in rotation on social media sites to ensure it reaches beyond your audience of readers.

Keep the information updated. Add a note to your calendar to revisit your most-popular pages to make sure the information is still accurate. Your audience is speaking: they like this content. Make sure it is the best possible representation of your business now and in the future.

Now the Fun Begins

Keep this book around and refer to it often. *Master Content Marketing* will be there for you if you struggle with a piece of content you're working on. Keep it nearby for inspiration, guidance, and support as you work to create content that builds your authority and your business.

See below, and be sure to register for all the additional educational materials I've created for you. I can't wait to hear about the content you create!

Master Content Marketing with Extra Tools and Resources

When you register for the free content marketing materials I've created for you, you'll get extra resources to help you apply the information in this book. It's easy and fast — and absolutely free.

Go to MasterContentMarketing.com/bonus to sign up.

SECTION 4

Appendices

Master Content Marketing Extras

Appendix is a funny name, isn't it? We know our appendix as that "extra" organ we were given at birth that serves a purpose but can — if it gives us any trouble — be removed, and we can go on without it.

The appendices that follow are extras I hope you'll find useful. In the first one, you'll find my Website Content Action Plan. If you're just starting a new website, the plan will help you map out the content you need in the early days of your site.

The second appendix gathers all the checklists from the main content marketing section in one place, so you can refer to them with just a glance.

In the third appendix, I've got some advice for editing your content when you need to do the editing work by yourself.

In the fourth appendix, my content marketing friends and colleagues generously share some encouraging words and helpful tips that will keep you motivated as you join the ranks of content marketers around the globe.

And finally, I've included some ways you can continue to learn about this topic in the final appendix at the end of the book.

APPENDIX 1
A Website Content Action Plan

If you're just starting a website and want to use content marketing to promote it, you may wonder exactly how much content you need to create in order to start seeing results. And by results, I mean action: we want people to find, read, enjoy — *and act on* — what we write.

And if you have an established website, you may wonder if you've got the right content in the right places. This appendix is written primarily for people who are putting together a new site. But if your site is already launched, read it to confirm you've got all your bases covered.

Here, we'll review the essential content elements every website should have in place. But I'm going to speak about it differently than you may have seen before.

Because when it comes right down to it, the most gut-wrenching part of creating a website is that moment when you decide to make it live. You work backstage with the curtains closed, putting everything into place. At some point, you have to draw back those curtains and let the audience see what you've been putting together. Your heart pounds, your palms sweat, and the spotlight blinds you. But you do it.

What I'm going to recommend here is that you draw back the curtains *as early as possible*. Get this daunting moment over with quickly. The longer you work behind the scenes with the curtains closed, the more excessive emotional energy you invest in your website. And the more nervous you become about revealing it.

Instead, think about creating what at Rainmaker Digital we like to call a "minimum viable website." This is a site that has the basics in place and serves as a foundation for everything you'll build on it in the future.

Here's the thing — websites aren't like the book you're holding right now. Websites aren't a project with a beginning and an end. They're fluid, organic, and always changing and growing.

Accept this early on, and you'll find it much easier to approach your content as a work in progress. Perfectionism will have less of a hold on you because you'll embrace the fluid nature of the product you're creating.

How to Approach Your Website in Phases

New websites are less overwhelming to tackle if you approach them in phases. The first phase includes the bare minimum pages you need to have in place to launch a new website to the world. The only goal is to get these few pages in place and *make it live*.

As an aside, let's state the obvious here so you can rest easy as you work on Phase 1. When you finally find the courage to draw back the curtains and reveal those initial pages you've put together, there's a very good chance that the seats in the auditorium will be … almost empty. Oh sure, you may peer out and see a handful of family members and friends sprinkled around in the dark. And they may be clapping wildly for your work! But the people you really want to attract to your website — the ones you are going to write content for — are completely absent.

That's because in the beginning, the search engines haven't found you. And although this may be frustrating at first, I'm going to ask you to try to see the upside of this situation.

In the beginning, when you're first putting your site together, it's wonderful to fly under the radar for a few months.

Here's the thing: when we're starting anything new, we can count on making all sorts of beginner mistakes. Our Home page will feature a glaring spelling error. One of the links in our sidebar won't work. We'll accidentally publish a piece of content before it's ready. We've *all* done these things — even the most experienced content marketers among us.

Making these kinds of mistakes when the audience consists of your friends and family is a blessing in disguise. You may wish you had a larger audience. But not when you flub up that link in the first line of your latest blog post! When that happens, take it from me — you're pretty happy that there aren't many people around to notice.

Phase 1: Essential for Launch

The bare minimum amount of content you need to have in place before you launch your new site are your Home page, About page, and Contact page. These pages are "evergreen" content marketing — you'll write them once and won't need to change them much over time.

Let's talk about the goals for each one. If your site has been around for a while, use this section to confirm that these three pages are meeting the goals you should have for them.

Your Home Page

Your Home page is the place people land when they type your web address into their browser. It's a front door to your business online. And that door should communicate — in just a few seconds — what visitors need to know about the business inside. Your Home page sets the stage for what's to come.

If your Home page works well, there's a good chance visitors will engage with your site. The scary part is, if your home page doesn't work well, they may visit once and never come back. When your Home page features the important elements we'll go over here, your business will be seen as trustworthy and authoritative. You'll make an A+ first impression, and that impression will last.

The first decision you'll want to make is whether you'll feature a static, unchanging Home page or use a blog or podcast with constantly updating content as your Home page. If you don't have a blog or podcast right now, this decision will be easy. You'll simply create a static Home page that explains what visitors will find on your site.

If you already have blog content or podcast episodes, you may want to use this content as your Home page. Why would you use a content page as your Home page?

- Blogs and podcasts feature your most recent content.
- If you talk about content that's time sensitive, you want people to see your most up-to-date information.
- You can feature several posts or podcast episodes and give the visitor a choice between different types of content.

It's not a bad way to handle a Home page, but I recommend you find a way to incorporate some of the static Home page components we'll talk about below. They'll help orient visitors and establish your authority early on.

There are advantages to using an unchanging Home page, and the most important one is that you have plenty of room to make a great first impression.

Why else would you want to have a static Home page?

- You might have specific offers you want to make on this high-traffic page.
- You have a welcome video you want to feature.
- Your site is complex and you need to orient visitors and help them choose a path through your information.

Either way — whether you show content on your Home page or use a static page — you'll want to answer these three important questions that are running through the minds of your site visitors when they land on your page:

- Where am I?
- Is this website worth my time?
- Can I trust this business?

Unlike an office, our websites don't have a human receptionist to help guide new visitors when they first enter your business. There's no one to guide your customer's journey as they come into your space. That's the job of your Home page. Help them feel welcome by answering their topmost questions right away.

Home Page Must-Haves

Display an easy-to-read site name and tagline. Your site visitors have just typed text into a browser or clicked on a link. Their most basic question is, "Am I in the right place?" Reassure them by featuring a clear site name on your Home page in an easy-to-read font. Use a tagline — a short phrase or sentence that highlights the benefits your business offers. Make it visually prominent and easy to find and read.

Show them what you've got for them. Think of your Home page like the display window at the front of your shop on Main Street. You want to entice people inside and let them know what they'll find there. So you find the most-engaging samples of wares you have, and you feature those in the front window to make people walking down the street want to open your front door and step inside your business. On your Home page, you want to entice those who are browsing the web to click to enter your online business. Use words or graphics to display the best of what you offer.

Establish authority early on. As of this writing, there are 993,565,287 sites online. That's just shy of a billion websites. Why should we trust your business over the other

993,565,286 out there? Let site visitors see why they should trust you — share the years you've been in business, your professional experience, the solutions your offer, and testimonials from happy customers.

Let's move on to the next essential Phase 1 page: your About page.

Your About Page

When people land on a site, they want to know who's behind it. Yes, they may be able to read a short bio after your latest post. But they often want to know more about the person or people behind the content they're enjoying. They want to know if your company is a good fit for them, so they're looking for an overview of who you are, what you offer, and who you help.

Make sure that your About page contains these key elements (and in this order):

Who you serve. Start with a compelling headline and let them know they're in the right place. Describe the ideal customer you like to serve, and do it in a way that they'll recognize themselves when they read the copy.

Who you are. After you've talked about *them,* then you can say who *you* are, or talk more about your business. This is where you can brag about awards your business has won, recognition you've received, licenses or certifications you hold, etc.

What you offer. Briefly describe (and add links) to the solutions you offer, whether they're products or services. This is also a perfect place to add testimonials from satisfied customers.

How to stay in touch. If you have email marketing set up, you may add an opt-in form to your Home page. Consider adding one on your About page, too. If people like what they've read about you and your business, they may want to stay in touch. Give them an easy way to do so right on your About page.

Your Contact Page

The next page you'll want to have in place before you launch is a Contact page. When your site visitors are ready to take the next step, they'll want to know how to get in touch with you.

Warning: don't post your email address on your contact page. Why? Because there are sketchy companies out there who troll web pages and scoop up email addresses. They sell those addresses to companies who will flood your inbox with spam. To protect your email address, use a contact form that will send responses to your inbox. Depending on the platform your website is built on, you'll either have a built-in contact form, or you can add one by using an inexpensive or free plugin. It's an extra step, but it will protect your email address from spam email you don't want.

Some people with online businesses are hesitant to include a phone number and mailing address on their Contact page. I believe it builds trust and confidence when people see that your business is "real" enough to have a phone number and a physical location, even if that location is a rented mailbox. And you don't have to post your mobile phone number — get a number online with Google Voice or Skype and set it up to take voice mail messages.

3-2-1, Launch

Once you have your Home, About, and Contact pages in place, you are ready to launch your new site. Really! There's no reason to wait. Get this step over with and continue to build your site on this foundation.

There's nothing to be lost and much to be gained by launching as soon as possible. Search engines use a site's "age" as part of their ranking signals. Make your site live early so you can start the timer and allow search engines to begin counting your site's age.

If you find you have extra time and energy, you can begin working on what's outlined in the next section — Phase 2.

Phase 2: Nice-to-Have (When There's Time)

The website element we'll cover in this section is nice to have in place for your site's launch, but isn't strictly necessary. You can work on it either before launch or after — it doesn't really matter. As we talked about in the previous section, it's more important to make your site live, so don't let the lack of what we're about to talk about hold you back from launching.

The next important element to get in place on your website is your content.

Content marketing is at the heart of this book, of course, and is what we covered in *Master Content Marketing*. In addition to Home, About, and Contact, you'll want to add a content page to your website's navigation.

Your content can take many forms. Written content is the most common type. Most people call it a blog, but there are still plenty of people who have no clue what the word "blog" means. If that's the case for the audience you'd like to reach with your content, don't be afraid to call it something else.

On some websites, the blog falls under a navigation item called "Articles." I have also seen it called "Resources," "Magazine," "News," "Information," and more. Think about your audience, decide what will resonate with them, and call your written content whatever makes the most sense to the people you want to reach.

What About Audio and Video?

Written content isn't your only option for a content page. If you enjoy creating audio, consider committing to publishing a podcast. Podcast content is convenient for your listener and highly portable — it's the only content type that can be consumed while driving, gardening, cooking dinner, or otherwise multitasking.

Some people use video as their primary vehicle for content. You can post a series of "talking head" videos, tutorial videos, or graphic, text-only videos.

The only drawback to audio and video content is that search engines have not yet come up with a way to index the content they contain to make them easier to find online. You can add categories, tags, and descriptions to audio and video content, and this can help. You can also take the extra step of having a transcription service turn your audio and video content into words. Publishing those words with your podcast or video content will help search engines to understand what it's about.

If you don't have pages and pages of content, don't let it hold you back from launching your website. In a perfect world, your content page will have a few posts, podcasts, or videos in place before you launch your site. But if you need to wait until after your site is live, that's fine. Search engines *love* content, and if you want to attract people to your website, frequently updated content is a highly effective way to draw them in.

Phase 3: After Launch

Most readers of this book will have a commerce element to their sites. You'll have a page where you want to allow transactions to happen. This could be called many different things: "Shop," "Store," "Order Now," "Members," "Products," and more. Just as I recommended for your content page, choose a commerce page name that will make sense to the audience you want to reach.

And remember, commerce doesn't have to mean the exchange of money. The word commerce comes from Latin, and at its heart it means "trading together." If you are looking for volunteers, or votes, or community action of some kind, set up a commerce page, call it something appropriate, and ask people to take action there.

This page can most definitely be set up after you launch your site. In fact, it might be preferable to wait a bit before setting it up. If your online presence is brand-new, take some time to get to know the people you're trying to attract to your business. Create content and begin sharing it. See how people react to it and respond to it — doing so will set you up for success once you're ready to ask for the sale.

How Often Should You Publish Content?

In Chapter 13, we talked about how often you should publish your content. The bottom line? *Aim for consistent quality.*

> *Content marketing results happen in proportion to the quality of the content you publish.*

How often can you realistically publish well-written, helpful, entertaining content? I'm going to bet that it's more often than you think right now. Review Chapter 13, which shares my system for making content creation easier (and more fun). It will help you form a "content habit" that will make content creation a natural part of your weekly schedule.

APPENDIX 2
Content Marketing Checklists

In this appendix, you'll find the checklists that I added to the end of the chapters that form the heart of this book. They cover how to think about, plan, and produce high-quality content marketing that attracts a profitable audience to your business.

Here's my best advice from each section at a glance.

The Efficient Approach to Marketing Your Business with Content: A Checklist

☐ **Recognize that it's a journey, not a destination.** The results from content marketing happen when you create compelling information consistently over time. When you set yourself up for success, you'll look forward to this creative task.

☐ **Embrace a "lazy" approach.** The "lazy" approach means making content creation easier by setting up a frictionless environment for getting your work done. "Lazy" = efficient and smart!

☐ **Find a place where you're physically comfortable.** Make it somewhere you can count on being able to work most days.

☐ **Use the best light for you.** Identify the lighting you prefer, and find a way to reproduce it consistently.

☐ **Put everything you need within arm's reach (or a few clicks).** Keep it all at hand so you don't interrupt your work session looking for something you're missing.

☐ **Identify your most creative time of day.** Take it from me; it's much easier to do creative work when you're working inside your most creative time of day. Pinpoint your ideal time, and block out part of it for content creation.

☐ **Don't judge. Just do.** Like an artist, incorporate a warm-up period where you write about anything that comes to mind. This will help prepare your mind and body for the creative work to come.

How to Plan Your Content: A Checklist

Use the checklist below to plan the content you'll create:

☐ **Build a category plan to guide you.** Think about your readers and what they'll want to understand and master within your larger topic.

☐ **Aim for eight to ten categories total.** If you're just starting out, choose four or five essential categories, so you have room to expand over time.

☐ **Use language your audience uses.** Avoid jargon and aim for clarity in your category names and in all your written content.

☐ **Create a content idea library.** Choose one place to store your ideas. Include your category plan so you can keep your overall structure at the top of your mind. Use a tool you'll enjoy adding ideas to over time.

Who Are You Writing For? A Checklist

Serve up content for every step of your prospect's journey. Make sure you have plenty of content for beginners, and ample content for those who are at an intermediate or advanced level.

☐ **For beginning readers, answer What is ___?** Beginning content defines a topic and helps web searchers expand their understanding of the basics.

☐ **For intermediate readers, answer How Do I Do ___?** Intermediate readers want to know how to apply what they're learning to their lives and situations. "How-to" content fits perfectly into this category.

☐ **For advanced readers, answer How Do I Get Better at ___?** Advanced readers crave mastery. What content can you create that will help them get really good at your topic?

Headline: A Checklist

☐ **Don't be shy.** Your headline has an important job to do. It needs to pull readers out of their sleepy web-searcher state of mind and engage them in your content. Don't be afraid to take a slightly more "sales-y" approach for your headlines.

☐ **Practice makes perfect.** Plan to spend some time as a "headline machine," churning out many headline ideas until you have one that truly works.

☐ **Keep your headline tools close by.** These include your blank sheet of paper (or a blank document), a thesaurus, and your headline inspiration ideas. Optional: give yourself extra motivation to get your ideas down quickly by using a timer.

☐ **Use words your readers already use.** Avoid jargon or cleverness in headlines. Aim for clarity and use words your readers already use to describe their challenges.

☐ **Research keyword phrases, but don't feel obligated to use them.** It's more important that your headline "sell" your content: if a keyword phrase fits and sounds compelling, use it. If not, focus on crafting a headline that will get clicks, and use the keyword phrases in a subhead or the content itself.

First Sentence: A Checklist

Help your reader make the transition from your headline into your content with a first sentence that keeps them on the page, engaged in your content.

Master the opening sentence style that feels most comfortable to you, then explore another style. You don't want to bore your readers by starting all your articles the same way.

There are many ways to open an article. The styles covered in the First Sentence chapter were:

☐ **The Storyteller's Opening Sentence,** which takes the reader directly into a story that's in progress, right at a point of high drama.

☐ **The Pitch-Style Opening Sentence,** which combines an astonishing claim and promises a desirable result.

☐ **The Suspense-Creating Opening Sentence,** which makes a statement that builds curiosity that can only be tamed by reading the article.

☐ **The Compelling Question Opening Sentence,** which asks a question (not a yes-no question) that leaves the reader wondering what you mean — and wanting to read on to clear up their confusion.

☐ **The Surprising Statement Opening Sentence,** which makes a bold claim that will be backed up by the content that follows.

Think about your first sentence as an entity in and of itself. It has an important job to do — it needs to pull your reader from clicking on your headline into engaging in your content. Spend time crafting an opening sentence that will do this important job well.

Introduction: A Checklist

Remember, the goal of the introduction is to move your reader into the main part of your content like an on-ramp moves a driver onto a busy highway.

Aim to write an introduction that is no more than 20 percent of the total words in your article — and shorter is better.

Write with a voice that makes you sound like a friendly, approachable, knowledgeable mentor — not a stiff and unwelcoming hotshot know-it-all.

Use the tips here to craft an introduction that will get your readers up to speed and engaged in your article.

☐ **Defend the importance of the information you'll share.** Back it up with compelling facts and stories of real results.

☐ **Surprise your reader with something they don't know (and don't expect).** Make sure it's related to the main point you'll make in your article.

☐ **Present ideas that conflict with one another.** Set up a conflict in your introduction that will make your reader want to stay tuned so they can see how it's resolved.

☐ **Plop them in the middle or at the end of a good story.** Don't reveal how the story resolves, of course, but talk about the ending and use the rest of the content to build out how the story got there.

☐ **Combine repetition and the Rule of Three for a powerful effect.** Using the Rule of Three and repetition together helps your content sound confident and persuasive. Repeat concepts, repeat words, repeat arguments. It works.

☐ **Master the placement of the More tag.** The More tag is one more barrier some of your readers will need to get past so they can access your full content. Make sure the sentence directly before it is compelling enough to make them want to click "Read More."

Subheads: A Checklist

Well-written, engaging subheads rely on some of the same techniques used to write compelling headlines. Take another look at the extensive headlines chapter in this book and try some of them when you write your subheads.

Subheads have an additional job to do within your content. Here's how to make them work for you:

☐ **Make a promise that makes the reader want to know more.** Subheads need to promise clear benefits for the section they head up. Don't be clever: you'll just confuse your readers. Let your reader know why they should be interested in the section they're about to read.

☐ **Write for the dual readership path.** Some people will only skim your article and may decide to share it with their audience based on this cursory glance alone. Make sure your subheads tell an independent (and interesting) story in case they're all someone ever reads.

☐ **Format so they stand out.** Subheads shouldn't look like body copy, and they shouldn't look like headlines, either. They should be bolder and larger than body copy. Capitalize the first letter only and don't capitalize any other words.

Main Copy: A Checklist

Your main copy is what will go below your subheads. It doesn't include your summary or call to action.

☐ **Aim for speed.** Getting your main copy written is a matter of speed: aim for an "ugly" first draft and get it down and done as quickly as possible.

☐ **Tell stories.** They're not essential, but where they work to support your premise, share stories. Fill them with rich detail that includes as many of the five senses as you can.

☐ **Build your case.** Think of your subsections as arguments that you'll use to build your case, slowly but surely.

☐ **Try to keep articles under 1,500 words.** Give or take a few hundred words in either direction, this length gives you enough room to tell your story, make your point, and wrap it up within just a few minutes of your readers' time.

☐ **Use transition sentences.** Pull readers through your content by occasionally using transitional sentences that foreshadow what they're about to read.

☐ **Use short sentences and paragraphs.** Keep sentences short — avoid using "and" in the middle of a sentence. Keep paragraphs short: two-three sentences total, and sprinkle in the occasional one-sentence paragraph.

☐ **Insert bulleted lists.** When a sentence includes comma after comma, replace it with a bulleted list. Start each bullet with a consistent part of speech so they're easy to skim.

☐ **Insert block quotes or call-outs.** Highlight important concepts in your article by styling them as block quotes — text that's styled to stand out from other body copy.

Summary: A Checklist

Your summary moves your reader from learning about a topic to wanting to take action. It's a small — often quite short — transition that smoothly takes them from learning to doing. Here's how to write a summary that sounds effortless and natural:

- ☐ **Remember your beginning at the end.** Refer to a story you told, a headline phrase, or the main points made.

- ☐ **Remind the reader about what they learned.** Create a feeling of reciprocity by re-stating the knowledge you've shared.

- ☐ **Reinforce how they'll benefit from what they read.** Paint a picture of the future results your reader can expect once they apply what they've learned.

- ☐ **Establish reasons to take action.** The section that follows — your call to action — is where you're going to ask your reader for something in return for what you've just shared. Move your reader smoothly toward it by including a mention of why the action matters.

Marks of an Effective Call to Action: The Checklists

Let's review what you can do to write and design calls to action that get people to act! After all, you're putting a tremendous amount of effort into creating informative, helpful, entertaining content — you deserve to see the business benefits of all this work. The call to action is where the business benefits begin to happen.

Verbal Call to Action Checklist

Your verbal call to action has three parts: the headline, the offer copy, and the button or link.

- ☐ **The headline copy.** Emphasize specific benefits, not features. Ask "why?" to identify specific benefits you can highlight in your headline and body copy.

☐ **The offer copy.** Be clear, not clever. Ask directly and don't include anything here that could be confusing.

☐ **The button or link copy.** "I want to ___." Reinforce what the reader will gain when they take you up on your offer.

Visual Call to Action Checklist

☐ **Use a different color palette.** Use colors that are across the color wheel from what people usually see on your site.

☐ **Make it larger and bolder.** Use a larger text size so your call to action stands out from the rest of the copy on the page.

☐ **Surround it with space.** Add open space all around your call to action to "point" people's eyes to it.

☐ **Use a background or a border.** By surrounding your call to action with a different color, you're saying, "This is something different: pay attention."

☐ **Don't be afraid to repeat your call to action.** If your page is long, insert a call to action every couple of "screens" your reader needs to page through on their way to the bottom.

Think about your call to action like an on-site salesperson who's representing the best of what your business offers. Spend time making this important element stand out both verbally and visually.

It may seem like a lot of work, but your call to action truly is where business happens! Take care to ensure it's as strong and convincing as it can be so it will work for you day and night, drawing prospects and customers to your business.

A System for Publishing Great Content: A Checklist

☐ **Focus on creating less content, but higher-quality content.** There's always room for well-written and beautifully presented information — the best content rises to the top.

☐ **Spread your content creation process out over four days.** This gives you space and time to do your best work.

☐ **Day 1: Build Your Article Backbone.** Pick your topic and focus on writing an engaging headline and strong subheads.

☐ **Day 2: Fill in the Details.** Fill in the structure you created on Day 1 with all your main copy: focus on speed and aim for first-draft quality (remember, no one will see this stage).

☐ **Day 3: Polish and Prepare to Publish.** Do a careful read-through to proofread and polish your article. Spend some time formatting it for readability. And choose an image that will communicate and intrigue readers. (More on this in the next chapter.)

☐ **Day 4: Publish, Promote, and Propagate.** Use this final day to put your article into circulation on social media. Give it a good push on the day of publication, repeating your posts about it several times on the platforms you use. Then add it to your long-term social media promotions, so you continue to drive readers to your content over time.

Using Images: A Checklist

☐ **Search with a goal in mind.** Get clear on what you want to accomplish with the image you'll add to your content before you search.

☐ **Don't get in legal hot water by searching in the wrong place.** Make sure you have full rights to every image you use.

☐ **Explore free stock photos.** Be sure to follow any requirements for photo credits and links.

☐ **Buy stock images.** For a small fee, you can find the perfect image for the job in the vast archives of stock photo sites.

☐ **Create images yourself.** Use your phone's camera to begin recording the world around you, and consider using your unique images in your content.

☐ **Search like a pro.** Use the tips in Chapter 14 to make your image searches faster and more targeted, so you'll find the exact image you need in record time.

APPENDIX 3

How to Edit Your Content Like a Master

In a perfect world, we'd have an editor/proofreader at our beck and call to review all our content before it publishes.

I can hear you laughing! And I know well that most of us have neither the funds nor the time built into our content creation schedules to benefit from the finishing touches a great editor can provide.

The reality is that many of us have to edit our own content. This may seem like an impossible task, but in this section, I'm going to share a few techniques that will make it doable.

Build Time into Your Content Creation Schedule

In Chapter 13, where I shared my four-day content creation system, I showed you how you can divide your content tasks up and spread them out over time.

Ideally, this happens over several days, as outlined in that chapter. In some cases, though, you may need to fit the steps into a single day — deadlines loom, and you've got to do what you've got to do.

In that case, be sure to take a break and step away from your keyboard in between step 2 — writing your main copy, and step 3 — polishing the copy and getting it ready to publish.

It doesn't have to be a long break, but it does need to be a break. Switch your brain off or think about something unrelated. Give it a rest so you can return to your content and see it with fresh eyes. This is the absolute best way to pick up on errors or structural problems you didn't notice before.

Use Spell Check and Grammar Check, and Consider Paid Services

Most word processing programs have built-in spelling and grammar checkers. These won't take care of usage errors and aren't smart enough to tell you when your writing is unclear, but they can save you from glaring typos and potentially embarrassing grammar mistakes.

Paid services like Grammar.ly offer more in-depth help. They're always on and available for everything you write, whether it's on your computer or on the web.

Trade Editing and Proofreading Favors with Another Content Creator

If you have a friend who creates content, why not swap your newest posts and give each other's work a thorough read-through? It's not the same as a professional editor, but just getting a fresh set of eyes on your work should help.

Another Way to Create Content: Work with a Writer

If after all this you still feel deeply uncomfortable creating your content, don't despair. You could work with writers on the Copyblogger Certified Content Marketer page to create your content. Find that page at copyblogger.com/certified-content-marketers.

Or you may find a writer who you could barter services with — someone who needs some of the skills you already have.

Either way, use the concepts in this book to inform the work you do. Now that you've read *Master Content Marketing,* you'll know quality content marketing when you see it.

APPENDIX 4

Content Marketers Share Their Secrets

Back in 2010, I didn't consider myself a writer at all. But I knew good writing when I read it. Masterful writers inspired me and made me want to improve my skills.

Today, I'm lucky to count many of the people I read over the years as colleagues and friends. Before I wrapped up writing *Master Content Marketing*, I reached out to them to see if they'd share some words of wisdom with you.

They responded with tips, techniques, and encouragement you're going to love! Many thanks to:

- Jay Baer of Convince and Convert
- Sean D'Souza of Psychotactics
- Chris Ducker of ChrisDucker.com
- Kelly Exeter of KellyExeter.com
- Demian Farnworth of TheCopyBot
- Stefanie Flaxman, Editor-in-Chief of the Copyblogger blog, and chief quality monitor for the written content we create at Rainmaker Digital
- Jeff Goins of GoinsWriter.com
- Karyn Greenstreet of Passion for Business
- John Jantsch of Duct Tape Marketing
- Bernadette Jiwa of The Story of Telling
- Joanna Penn of The Creative Penn
- Darren Rowse of Problogger
- Courtney Seiter of Buffer
- Joanna Wiebe of Copyhackers

"What do you do to stay excited about your topic of choice after all these years? How do you keep yourself inspired?

One issue content marketers struggle with is how to keep their interest high even though they're writing about the same topic for months and years. Here's how master content marketers handle this challenge:

For **Darren Rowse,** it's about the people he serves:

"The thing that continually inspires me to create content for my blog and podcast is regularly meeting my readers both in person and online. Talking with a reader about the dreams that they have and the challenges that they face gives me both ideas for content but also renewed passion for my topic."

Bernadette Jiwa just has to imagine her readers:

"What excites me is the people on the other side of this computer screen I'm reading from as I type. People I have never met, from all over the world, in places I may never visit who are searching for something. And I have the opportunity to help them with nothing other than 101 keys and an Internet connection. Thinking about how the world used to be and that one person I might be able to reach is what keeps inspires me to keep going."

Chris Ducker's interactions with his audience fuel his content ideas:

"I stay excited about my topic of choice — and just inspired, in general — by hanging out with my audience and my community as much as I possibly can. I'm a big believer that if you listen to your audience and pay attention to what they are saying, your job as a content creator and a content marketer becomes even easier over the long haul."

For **John Jantsch,** empowering others with his content gives his work meaning:

"Most of what I write about comes from doing and helping others do, so what keeps it exciting for me is working with clients and training consultants to work with clients."

Joanna Wiebe gets inspired by what she finds in her inbox:

"I thrive on emails from people who are new to copywriting. All of their questions remind me that the stuff I may take for granted or think the whole world knows is actually pretty mysterious to a significant portion of the planet's seven billion people."

Demian Farnworth thrives on the novelty of new topics:

"The challenge of tackling a new subject, uncorking difficult problems, tackling new technology — that's how I stay excited: I conquer and move on."

Jay Baer knows that our ever-changing marketing environment will provide an endless stream of content inspiration:

"The great thing about creating content about marketing and customer service is that disruption never ends. There's always a new trend, a new best practice, a new case study. There is no end to the lessons and the learning."

For **Joanna Penn,** choosing a topic area that was broad enough to hold her interest for the long haul has made a difference:

"I made the mistake of making [my first two blogs] hyper-focused on one niche, where I soon became bored. But by opening up the focus of my blog to basically include anything on creativity — although it is specifically book and writing related for now at least — I was able to give myself unlimited scope."

Sean D'Souza excavates his topics to find new inspiration:

"I dig deep into the subject matter. I won't stay at the topic level. For example, I'll start with a topic like "headlines," but at a sub-topic level, I'll examine how to dig through your testimonials for great headlines. You have to be like a geologist, always digging."

And **Kelly Exeter** thrives on continuing her education:

"I read everything I can get my hands on in my area of interest. As long as I'm learning new things, I'm excited about what I am writing about (because I'm sharing what I'm learning) ... and that excitement comes through in my writing. The day I feel I have nothing left to learn, or I'm not interested in learning more, that's the day I know it's time to move on."

"How have you eliminated friction from your content creation process?"

In this book, we've talked about how to break down the content creation process into manageable pieces and to have a process for getting those pieces done. It's no surprise that the most prolific and skillful content creators I know have developed similar processes:

Sean D'Souza says:

"Friction is caused by doing everything together. I think of any project as a meal being prepared. The ingredients, the cutting, the cooking, the tasting, the plating, the garnish. They're all steps. And often they have to be done on different days. Friction comes from trying to do it all together and taxing your brain needlessly. Doing something from start to finish doesn't allow your brain to work out possibilities."

Joanna Wiebe supports her content creation process by gathering ideas and building a group of resources that are waiting for her when she sits down to write:

"I'm a compulsive clipper. When I come across particularly interesting anecdotes or data points online, I use my Airstory browser extension to clip them, tag them, and send them to my writing projects. Then when it's time to write a post, I filter my clips by tag, see which tags have the most clips, and choose the one with the most to write a post around. Then it's just a matter of outlining and writing, which both happen much faster once you've got the research in place."

Chris Ducker has a "content production assembly line" in place, where he batches his content creation. Smart! Why not write several articles, record several podcasts, and film several videos at once?

"The biggest thing for me ... is to batch. It doesn't matter if it's a podcast, or if it's a blog post — we'll write four, five, six posts all at the same time. And then we'll schedule them out over a period of time, based on whatever focus we've got that quarter or that month, whatever it is from a content distribution perspective."

For **Joanna Penn,** an article is just one piece of a larger whole. She starts with audio and spins each recording into multiple pieces of content marketing:

"I turn my podcast interviews into multiple pieces of content. I record 45 minute interviews via video Skype, which I turn into a video on YouTube, an audio podcast on iTunes and Stitcher, and then I get a transcript of it which becomes a blog post and is valuable for SEO. I then share those posts with links to the audio and video on social media, and schedule it into my social media queue. I use Speechpad.com for transcription and I have a VA who edits and loads it into the blog. So essentially, I get a whole lot of content from that one weekly interview."

John Jantsch plans ahead — way ahead. He and his team map out their core editorial themes for an entire year, which gives them plenty of time to think about how they'll approach a topic.

"Sounds pretty obvious, but my best efficiency hack is planning. We map out our core themes for the year and then create an editorial calendar around that. Having time to think about a topic is one of the best ways to eliminate friction for me."

Darren Rowse uses a system that's not unlike the one you learned in this book — spread your content creation out over several days so you can write the best-quality piece possible.

"I have slowly learned over the last 14 years that I work best when I divide my content creation process down into three parts and focus upon each separately at different times.

I allocate time firstly to generate ideas and plan what content I should create, secondly to create the content, and thirdly to complete and polish the content.

I'm no neuroscientist but suspect we use different parts of our brain for these three tasks and as a result sometimes get into trouble when we attempt to do all three in a sitting."

Kelly Exeter came to the same conclusion: content creation is easier (and the result is better) when you don't try to do it all in one sitting.

"I've stopped trying to write an entire post and press publish on the same day as this makes the content creation process very stressful and pressured. I have a big pile of ideas saved in my Evernote and once a month I sit down and bang out four very dodgy first drafts using the four ideas that most excite me at that time. That process then allows those four posts to marinate in my brain for a while so that when it comes time to write the second draft and take it to publication level, the words flow much more easily."

Jay Baer uses a process and sticks to his self-imposed deadlines (do you see a pattern here?):

"We build a content creation, syndication, amplification process for every type and piece of content we produce at Convince & Convert. The only way you can do this well without driving yourself crazy is to be consistent and adhere to process and deadlines with fervor."

Jeff Goins doesn't worry about friction — he worries about something else:

"Friction is always involved in creating anything of substance. I'm not scared of that. Friction is good. It means you're moving. I'm more concerned about inertia."

And **Karyn Greenstreet** recommends outlining your content, walking away, and coming back to it:

"I use a two-step process for content creation. The first step is to outline the content (whether it's a blog post, a book or a class design). This outline helps me to clarify what I want to focus on and where I need to do research. Then I let the outline sit for a week while my subconscious brain sorts out the words I'll need to express myself. The second step is to write out the content in full. Since my brain has been muddling through the outline for a week (or more!), the words flow easily."

"What traits do you consider to be hallmarks of quality in a piece of content? What makes content trustworthy?"

As content marketers, we're all aiming for the same goal — quality content that builds trust, attracts an audience, and grows our profits. It's reassuring to read similar answers to these questions, which seem to boil down to "emotion + facts = quality and trust."

Courtney Seiter says we should approach content creation with the highest of standards:

"In my mind, marketing content works best when it's held to the same standards of journalistic content. I most appreciate work that's bias-free (or at least owns up to any biases) and deeply researched with sources cited, and pieces that teach me something new, or advance the current thinking on a topic."

Chris Ducker says quality content starts with quality research:

"I think in terms of a quality piece of content, research is a given. You've got to be well researched in what you're doing, whether you're doing the research yourself or maybe you have an assistant helping you with it."

Karyn Greenstreet admires content that's focused and simple:

"If the writer can take a complicated topic and make it simple, if they can create content that's organized and focused, I would give up chocolate if it meant I could learn at their feet!"

John Jantsch says we should aim for an emotional reaction to the content we share:

"I don't always get there, but for me, if you can share useful information that also makes me feel some emotion — I don't care if it's anger or inspiration — making people feel something is the greatest form of influence."

Jeff Goins says we need to give people something to have an opinion about:

"The best writing has an argument. It's something people can and should disagree with. You serve no one when you write something so bland everyone would agree with it."

Stefanie Flaxman recommends tapping into your readers' beliefs:

"You'll establish trust when you demonstrate not only your expertise, but also validate your audience's beliefs. Messages within quality content deeply resonate with the reader. It's the type of content that teaches and also makes the reader think, 'Yes! That's what I believe to be true also.'"

Darren Rowse says building trust works both ways:

"Bob Burg famously said that people do business with those that they 'know, like, and trust.' I've heard many people take this quote and write that we need to create content that helps people to know, like, and trust us.

… The fastest way to make someone know, like, and trust us is to change their life in some way. Create content that solves a problem or a need and you go a good way to building trust.

The other advice I'd give is to create content that shows your readers that you know, like, and trust them.

- *Show your reader that you know them — their dreams, pain, challenges, language, etc.*
- *Show your reader that you like them — that you genuinely want to have a conversation with them and help them.*
- *Show your reader that you trust them — that you're willing to be vulnerable and tell your story."*

Joanna Wiebe recommends combining hard facts and a distinct writing style:

"Proof and voice. Proof — like data and examples — turns fluffy opinion pieces into good, readable content. Then you add voice, and that's where the magic happens, that's where good content becomes great. Proof makes you trustworthy, and voice makes you likable."

For **Demian Farnworth,** memorable content combines enduring themes and specific information:

"Great writing endures over the years because it touches upon the human condition. What makes it compelling is the narrative: the facts about an event, and why they matter. What makes it believable and trustworthy are the details: specific and unexpected."

As a respected book author, **Joanna Penn** has noticed that when it comes to books, "quality" is relative:

"Quality ... is essentially in the eyes of the beholder. I've learned this with books. There are some books that are considered literary works of genius that barely sell because people don't want to read that, and then a book like 50 Shades of Grey *sells 100 million copies, and people love it. So quality has to relate to what your audience wants."*

Sean D'Souza also endorses the idea that the best content has a recognizable voice:

"Trust comes from many sources, but one of the biggest trust factors in real life is knowing the other person. If you're not ready to talk about yourself, then I know nothing about you. It's harder to relate to people who have a paper bag over their heads."

Kelly Exeter agrees! Connecting with your audience is what makes your content memorable:

"Connection — usually gained through excellent storytelling — is what causes an article to really resonate ... and leads to it being shared widely."

And for **Jay Baer,** trust is built from four essential components:

"To me, there are four components of content trustworthiness: the earned credibility of the author; the depth and perceived authority of the content itself; the production quality of the content; and evidence of endorsement (i.e. social proof and other signals)."

"What weird tip can you share that you use to create effective content?"

After you've created content for a while, you may develop your own set of habits that work well for you. You just read about mine in this book. My colleagues have developed their own unique habits and methods which make content creation easier.

Darren Rowse says it's easier to tap into emotions if he writes with a soundtrack that inspires them:

"Sometimes when I write I find a playlist of aspirational, orchestral movie soundtracks on Spotify and I pump it up loud to get me in the mood to write.

This music has been composed with the intent of making moviegoers feel something. It engages the emotions, and I find that it puts me in a place that makes it easier to write from the heart."

Kelly Exeter says taking pen to paper helps her sort through her ideas:

"Write your first drafts longhand."

Sean D'Souza believes giving your brain time to rest makes you a better writer:

"Sleep. I sleep more than ever before. To create efficiency, I don't work harder — I sleep. I'll nap during the day, take weekends off. I'm on full charge when I work, or I don't work."

Joanna Wiebe finds that this specific writing technique makes her content stronger:

"Leave gaps. Readers and viewers need to have some questions left unanswered. If your whole argument is tied up neatly in a bow or if you hit on every single way to do X in your listicle, then what are they going to comment about?"

John Jantsch reads broadly to find concepts he can apply to his own content:

"I read articles or even books that are totally unrelated to my field looking specifically for crossover ideas I can apply."

Courtney Seiter takes inspiration from children's inherent curiosity:

"Be like a toddler: Ask 'why?' Again and again and again."

Chris Ducker shared a weird tip he uses to make recording video much easier. First off, he keeps it simple: he records video using his phone camera. And to avoid sounding scripted, he does this:

"I use sticky notes, and I usually have no more than three bullet points that I want to go over in a two-minute video. I just stick the sticky notes to the phone where I'm recording so that I'm not distracted by looking at myself on that reverse camera. I hit record, sit in front of it, and boom, two minutes later I'm done."

"If you could go back in time and grab your newbie content creator self by the shoulders, what crucial piece of advice would you pass along?"

Everyone starts somewhere, and my colleagues all remember their early days as content creators. If you're just starting out creating content, they have some advice for you in their answers to this question.

Joanna Penn urges you to take heart. Content marketing won't give you instant results, but over time you'll see the payoff:

"Everything takes time, so have patience. It's true that you will overestimate what you can achieve in a year, but in a few years' time, you will look back, and your life will have changed in unimaginable ways!"

Darren Rowse says practice makes perfect:

"Create something every day. The more you do it, the better you get."

Kelly Exeter recommends getting comfortable with expressing yourself:

"Stop trying to write like other people and just write like yourself!"

Jay Baer is a big believer in video content:

"Get better at video, faster."

Courtney Seiter says to be courageous!

"Be brave. Make yourself uncomfortable. The scariest stories to publish are the ones that will connect most with people and make you love writing all over again."

Jeff Goins urges you to cultivate your voice:

"Voice matters more than your topic. It's not just what you say. It's how you say it. Don't just pick a topic; find a worldview, a unique way of sharing your message. Say something worth disagreeing with."

Sean D'Souza realizes that success doesn't unfold in a straight line:

"People think that you go from good to great. Instead, you go from good to hopeless and then back to good before becoming great."

John Jantsch says it's not about you — it's about your reader:

"Make the reader the hero of your story and stop obsessing over how cute and witty your writing is (ouch, that was a bit cathartic!)."

Chris Ducker shares how you can avoid duplicating efforts by thinking about how you'll repurpose your content from the very beginning:

"If I could go back in time and give my newbie content creator self a bit of advice it would be to repurpose, repurpose, and repurpose. Back when I first started creating content,

boy oh boy, was I wasting time. I'd create a piece of content, or rather I'd create a blog post, and then I would record a podcast about the same thing, and then I might shoot a video about the same topic, and obviously I was spinning my wheels like crazy, wasting my time. Now almost every piece of content that I create is repurposed in some way, shape, or form."

Karyn Greenstreet says just get started (despite your fear) and let momentum carry you the rest of the way:

"Just write. The consistent habit of writing is crucial. Waiting for 'inspiration' will kill you. The hardest part of writing is the first 15 minutes. If you just write for 15 minutes, I guarantee you'll keep writing that day. Even if you feel empty, even if you feel afraid, even if you don't know what to say, just write."

And finally, **Joanne Wiebe** says … relax! And have fun:

"Don't take yourself too seriously! For the first years of my blogging life, I counted comments and shares on every post, which sucked all the joy out of writing for a living.

Have fun! Don't count! Don't compare! Let yourself screw up, and then do it all over again. Even if it chases away people who said they loved you!

I've learned to evolve and let go of ideas about 'who Joanna is.' Writing content helps me explore who I am and what my brand is all about. Taking myself so seriously only hurt that discovery process."

I think "don't take it too seriously" is a great way to end this appendix, and this book. Mastering content marketing can be one of the most creatively fulfilling things you'll ever do. Don't forget to have fun!

When you're ready to learn more about content marketing, use the resources in the final appendix to continue your education.

APPENDIX 5

Content Marketing Tools, Websites, Software, and Templates

The books and websites below have inspired my content marketing journey — read them to learn more about content production, writing strong content, and the business of blogging.

Ongoing Education, Websites, Software, and Tools

The company I work for, Rainmaker Digital, is the creator of the Rainmaker Platform. We call it the smarter solution for digital marketing and sales, because it includes everything a content marketer needs to build a robust online presence.

Check out the Rainmaker Platform here: rainmakerplatform.com

We also offer advanced content marketing training, which I help create. I'd love to see you in one of our programs!

Our Authority Advanced Content Marketing Training program is for anyone who's using content marketing to promote a business, an idea, or a cause — whether it's their own business or their clients' businesses.

Learn more about Authority here: my.copyblogger.com/join-authority.

Our Certified Content Marketer Program offers training for professional writers who offer content marketing services. This is our most advanced content marketing training and it offers the opportunity to apply for certification once the program is complete. People who receive certification are listed on our Certified Content Marketer page at Copyblogger.

Learn more about Certification here: copyblogger.com/certified-content-marketers.

And of course, every weekday we publish valuable, interesting, highly readable (if I may say so myself) content about content marketing on Copyblogger.com. The Copyblogger website uses our online marketing software, the Rainmaker Platform.

If you're creating content for your own business, pay a visit to my website, BigBrandSystem.com. You'll discover how to combine marketing, design, and content to create a recognizable brand that attracts customers and builds your bottom line.

Which Books to Read Next

Content Chemistry: An Illustrated Handbook for Content Marketing, by Andy Crestodina.
    Andy is an engaging writer, and this is a beautifully designed book. He includes innovative ways to approach your content creation process and lots of ideas for multiplying the impact of one piece of content by using it in various formats.

Everybody Writes: Your Go-To Guide to Creating Ridiculously Good Content, by Ann Handley.
    Ann is an empathetic writer who's passionate about helping people — even those who come late to the writing game — become confident, competent writers.

Get Content Marketing Templates and More Resources

Register to get access to content marketing templates, tools, and resources that will make mastering content marketing fun and easy. Pick them up at MasterContentMarketing.com/bonus

Where to From Here?

My wish for you is that mastering content marketing will open up new doors for you. I hope you'll discover:

- You're more creative than you may have realized
- Your words can influence people's actions
- Your disciplined approach to content creation has a positive impact on other areas of your life

Now that you've finished reading this book (thank you), I have to confess that on its own, this book is completely worthless. The only value comes when you apply what you've learned here. The best education happens not by *reading* but by *doing*.
    I hope you'll take the strategies you've learned here and begin applying them on your website. The sooner you start sharing your content with the world, the sooner you'll be able to attract a profitable audience that will build your business and help spread your ideas.

Acknowledgments

To my husband, Jim, who has offered his unwavering belief in my capabilities, even when I wasn't so sure of them myself. Thanks for helping me giggle through all the hard parts.

To the Book Factory community on Big Brand System. I put my first attempts at writing a book in front of you, and you responded with helpful guidance, eagle-eyed proofreading, and all the encouragement a brand-new author could ever need. Thank you.

To Jeff Goins, who wrote me the shortest email of the year when he replied "Me" to my question about who might be able to coach me through writing my first book. Your idea to make our coaching sessions public on our ZeroToBook.fm podcast was brilliant. I'll be forever grateful for your guidance and encouragement as I worked on what I hope will be the first of many books. (Hear how this book was born at ZeroToBook.fm.)

And finally, to my friends and colleagues at Rainmaker Digital. I learned content marketing from you, and I'm honored to count myself as part of a team I admire and respect. I continue to learn from you every day. Goonies forever!

About the Author

Pamela Wilson has been helping people get their ideas out into the world since 1987. She started her career as a marketing consultant and graphic designer and began her online business — BigBrandSystem.com — in early 2010.

In 2014, she joined the team at Rainmaker Digital — publishers of the Copyblogger blog. Copyblogger is the industry-standard content marketing resource on the web. Pamela manages the Copyblogger editorial team and Rainmaker Digital's content marketing education programs: Authority and the Copyblogger Certified Content Marketer program.

Pamela lives in Nashville, TN.

CPSIA information can be obtained
at www.ICGtesting.com
Printed in the USA
BVOW08s0041150318
510168BV00005B/276/P